CREATION/EVOLUTION
SATIRICON:
CREATIONISM BASHED

A freethinker's view of the modern
conflict between religious fundamentalism
and rational thought...a battle that could
have profound effects on public education
in America

BY

ROBERT S. DIETZ
&
JOHN C. HOLDEN

Dedication

This impious work is dedicated to the Roman satirist of the first century Gaius Petronius who about 60 A.D. wrote the first *Satiricon*, of which only fragments remain today — and which is probably just as well. He was appointed *Arbiter Elegantiae,* a title bestowed by Tacitus, to the Emperor Nero which made him *the* authority in matters of taste, manners and elegance. Petronius' opus concerned satyrs as well as satire so his manuscript is sometimes mislabeled, we believe, as the *Satyricon.* Just to put the matter straight, the present work is limited to satire — and religious satire at that.

Nero, of course, had little or no (mostly no) manners but this was offset by an abundance of taste (unfortunately all bad). As for his other sterling (read tarnished) qualities, Nero was about as good and loving as the Great God Jehovah of the Old Testament. Petronius himself, however, sets the mood for our palimpsest *Satiricon* with his classic observation, *"Detexit quo dolose Vaticinandi furore sacerdotes mysteria illis saepe ignota, audactur publicant".*

This book is not for everybody. An IQ of at least 80 is required for its understanding. If you don't qualify your money will be refunded cheerfully (read reluctantly).

Do you ever wonder what life is all about? Where you go, if anywhere, after you die? Will you go to Heaven or Hell? Can you ask for a refund if you don't like your afterlife? In this book we promise to solve none of these eternal questions.

About the Authors

Robert S. Dietz is a secular humorist and an emeritus professor in geology at Arizona State University in Tempe, Arizona. He has published extensively on marine geology, plate tectonics and meteorites.

John C. Holden is a geologist, freelance illustrator and humorist. He currently resides in rural northcentral Washington State seeking truth and avoiding those who have found it.

Both authors are Christians of the common garden variety. They were only born once and are nominal Episcopalians in the sense that this is the church they do not go to.

Woe Be Unto Thee

Library of Congress Catalog
Card Number: 87-070647

ISBN: 0-939075-02-4

© R.S. Dietz and J.C. Holden, 1987

Upon this rock we built our book.

Published by:

The BOOKMAKER
Star Route 38
Winthrop, WA 98862
(509) 996-2576

This book may be obtained directly from the publisher.
$9.95, plus $2.00 shipping and handling.

i

Preface

This book is intended to be a serious satire on the creation/evolution controversy, a subject which has attracted considerable media attention in the past few years. It is a prime example of ongoing conflict between science and religion—not mainstream religion but that of the fundamentalists, evangelicals and radical right. Most Christians and most churches (the real majority, if not the Moral Majority) have accommodated their theology with the advancing scientific understanding of nature but fundamentalist views remain archaic and set in concrete.

Unfortunately when scientists write critiques of creationism they are interacting among themselves and not reaching lay audiences. It is not easy to reach the fundamentalists because many of them are minimally literate and do not read above the comic book level. Offering scientific evidence is useless as this is fully negated by their blind faith even though evolution is as firmly established as the earth being a sphere and not flat. Religionists prefer fantasy to reality.

Knowledgeable people are well aware that the Bible is not a scientific or an accurate historical treatise but rather largely mythical, metaphorical, legendary, poetic, theological and moral. But all people are not knowledgeable. Recent Gallup poll surveys show that 50 percent of Americans believe that Adam and Eve really existed, 44 percent believe that God created the earth between six and ten thousand years ago, 50 percent accept the reality of the Great Flood and Noah's Ark and some 80 percent believe that man was specially created. Some 40 percent accept the Bible as inerrant and infallible and denounce evolution. Estimates on the number of fundamentalists in the U.S.A. run from about 30 million to more than 70 million so that they are a formidable voting block. Theocracies of the far right have sprung up in various parts of the world (e.g., the Shiite Muslims of Iran) and are becoming ever more dominant. They pose a serious destabilizing influence because differences between theocracies are settled by wars not reason.

This book consists of five parts:
1) Historical and Modern Background
2) Creationism and Fundamentalism
3) Creationism and the Physical Sciences
4) Evolution and Creationism
5) The Philosophy of Science

In each of these parts there are a series of mini-essays, cartoons, aphorisms, and definitions. An effort is made to provide light and humorous reading. In 1925 at the Scopes "Monkey Trial" in Tennessee, the satirist, H.L. Mencken wrote, "One good horse-laugh is worth a thousand syllogisms." This book is written in that vein.

Acknowledgements

We thank Mitchell Woodhouse, Mike Irwin, Brad Archer, and Jamie Busch for their assistance in the preparation of this work.

– CONTENTS –

Disclaimer

This book complies with the balanced treatment, even-handed, fair is fair laws of most states with some exceptions. Equal space has been given to evolution and to that version of special creation called biblical creationism. This book treats evolution as "just a theory" but a damn good theory at that — and also as a fact. Equal space has also been accorded between astronomy and astrology, chemistry and alchemy, and psychiatry and phrenology.

This book has been unable to obtain the imprimatur of the boards of education in the states of Texas, Arkansas, Tennessee, and Louisiana. School children in those states are instructed to discard this book before reading. This also applies to exceptional (read idiot) children with IQ's below 80.

This opus is not suitable for native americans of the Navajo or Hopi nations. Our attempt to obtain their versions of special creation was entirely too successful. We could not accommodate the 204 versions, so in fairness omitted all. The authors extend regrets.

This volume was printed entirely on unrecycled paper. Great swaths of virgin forests were cut down and the land devastated in both Sequoia and Yellowstone National Parks. Thousands of cute little furry animals were left homeless. So treat this book with respect!

This book is a work of fiction. Any resemblance to any person living or dead is purely coincidental. All characters depicted are over 18 years of age.

PART 1

CREATION/EVOLUTION: HISTORICAL AND MODERN BACKGROUND

HALLELUJAH DARWIN!

In 1859, Charles Darwin published his landmark treatise *Origin of Species* positing that life slowly evolved from the simple to the complex by natural selection and survival of the fittest. The immediate effect was electrifying, like a plow striking an anthill, causing the pious to scurry about in great confusion as it threatened their cherished beliefs. But Darwin's thesis was quickly accepted by the scientific community because it was extraordinarily powerful in explaining the mysteries of life in the world around us. Answers to thousands of puzzling questions yielded to this revolutionary concept. This British naturalist left an enduring legacy by plowing under the Garden of Eden and completing the work begun by Copernicus, Kepler, and Galileo when they destroyed the "heavenly firmament." The quick acceptance by the Church of England (Anglican) of Darwinism was confirmed by his burial in Westminister Abbey in 1882 — even over the objection of Queen Victoria. This was not so for the reactionary and entrenched fundamentalist churches which reject the concept of evolution even to this day.

Darwin was a gentle and retiring man who deigned not to defend his ideas in public. The relationship of evolution to man is avoided until its brief mention in one paragraph at the very end of his book. There he acknowledges that his theory may throw some light on the origin of man and his ancestry. But he was not unaware of the impact of his writings on man's place in nature, for in 1857, Darwin wrote to Wallace (the "co-author" of the evolution concept): "You ask whether I shall discuss man...I think I shall avoid the whole subject, as it is surrounded with prejudices; although I fully admit that it is the highest and most interesting problem for the naturalist."

William Jennings Bryan, prosecutor at the Scopes "Monkey Trial" in Tennessee, 1925. Bryan, a fundamentalist, believed in the Rock of Ages but not the age of rocks. Said he: "I would rather be right than President." Fortunately, he was neither -- although he ran for the presidency three times.

1860 - 1925

Although Darwin was reticent, some of his colleagues were not, especially Thomas Huxley who so championed Darwinism that he became known as "Darwin's Bulldog." At a meeting of the British Association for the Advancement of Science, he engaged in a classic debate on evolution with Bishop Samuel Wilberforce of Oxford also known as "Soapy Sam" for his saponaceous sermons. Said Huxley, "If I had to choose, I would prefer to be a descendant of a humble monkey rather than a man who employs his knowledge and a eloquence in misrepresenting those who are wearing out their lives in a search for the truth."

The growing acceptance of evolution in the U.S. was interrupted in 1925 by the infamous Tennessee "Monkey Trial" in a test case which attracted world wide attention. A high school science teacher, John Scopes, was accused of teaching evolution in violation of a recently enacted state law. The trial pitted the wily and liberal lawyer Clarence Darrow against the silver-throated fundamentalist William Jennings Bryan, thrice unsuccessful candidate for President who "believed in the Rock of Ages but not the age of rocks." Said Darrow, "You are proposing setting man against man and creed against creed until, with banners flying and beating your drums, we are marching backward into the glorious ages of the 16th century, when bigots lighted faggots to burn men who dare to bring any intelligence, enlightenment and culture to the human mind." And as an after remark he teased, "When I was a boy, I was told that anyone could become president. Now I believe it."

In the end Bryan prevailed. Scopes was found guilty and fined $100. The law remained on the books and was not rescinded until 1967. It was, however, a Pyrrhic victory — Bryan won the battle but lost the war. Tennessee became stereotyped as a backward state inhabited by retarded hillbillies. Bryan's bible-thumping fundamentalism was widely ridiculed especially in the satirical reporting by the likes of H. L. Mencken of the Baltimore Sun. Bryan, in a state of shock, died a few days after the trial's end.

For several decades following the "Monkey Trial," rationality appeared to be once again in ascendency. But in recent years the crazies have once again appeared at the gate clamoring for creationism in our schools. It would seem that the dissemination of intelligence cannot keep pace with the propagation of ignorance.

Excerpt from the testimony of Dudley Malone in defense of John Scopes at the Dayton, Tennessee "Monkey Trial", 1925:

"If the court please, Your Honor...whether William Jennings Bryan knows it or not he is a mammal, he is an animal, and he is a man...I know, Your Honor, that Mr. Bryan believes. But he is not the only one who believes; he is not the only one who believes in God; and he is not the only one who believes in the Bible...

"The difference between the theological mind and the scientific mind is that the theological mind is closed because religious truths are final. But the scientist says, 'No, the

Bible is the book of revealed religion, with rules of conduct and with aspirations. Take the Bible as guide, as an inspiration, as a set of philosophies and preachments in the world of theology.'

"Mr. Bryan says: The Bible contains the truth; if the world of science can produce any truth or facts not in the Bible, as we understand it, then destroy science, but keep our Bible. And we say: Keep your Bible. Keep it as your consolation, keep it as your guide, but keep it where it belongs, in the world of your own conscience, in the world of your individual judgment, in the world of the Protestant conscience that I heard so much about when I was a boy. Keep your Bible in the world of theology where it belongs, and do not try to tell an intelligent world and the intelligent of this country that such books written by men, who knew none of the accepted fundamental facts of science, can be put into a course of science, because what are they doing here?

"I feel that the prosecution here is filled with a needless fear. I believe that if they withdrew their objection and heard the evidence of our experts, their minds would not only be improved, but their souls would be purified. I believe that our science teachers are God-fearing men who are giving their lives to study and observation and to the teaching of the young. Are the teachers and scientists of this country in collusion to destroy the morals of the

"Even if Darwin is right, Bishop Wilberforce, let's hope it doesn't get around too much."

The flattened muzzle of the English bulldog, better known for its tenacity than its IQ, apparently evolved from chasing after parked cars.

children to whom they have dedicated their lives? Are preachers the only ones in America who care about our youth? Is the church the only source of morality in this country?

"I would like to say something for the children of the country... For God's sake, let the children have their minds open — close no doors to their knowledge; shut no doors from them. Make the distinction between theology and science. Let them have both. Let them both be taught. Let them both live. Let them both be revered. But we come here to say that the defendant is not guilty of violating this law. We have a defendant whom we contend could not violate this law. We have a defendant whom we can prove by witnesses whom we have brought here, and are proud to have been brought here, to prove, we say, that there is no conflict between the Bible and whatever he taught...

"Are our children to know nothing about science except what the church says they shall know? We have no fears about the young people of America. I feel that children of this generation are wiser than many of their elders. I have never seen harm in learning and understanding, in humility and open-mindedness. And I have never seen clearer that need than now when I see the attitudes of the prosecution, who attack and refuse to accept the information which expert witnesses offer to give them...

"Mr. Bryan has referred to this as a duel. But does he mean a duel in which the defendant shall be strapped to a board and he alone shall carry the weapon? Truth, Your Honor, is our only weapon...The truth does not need the law. The truth is no coward. The truth does not need the forces of government. The truth does not need Mr. Bryan. The truth is imperishable, eternal and immortal, and needs no human agency to support it."

At one stage of his life, Darwin had wanted to become a minister, but just as he qualified to take up a position, he made his pivotal voyage on the *Beagle*. Eventually he became disillusioned with religion.

In his autobiography he wrote this: "I gradually came to disbelieve in Christianity as a divine revelation.... This disbelief crept over me at a very slow rate, but at last was complete."

Th. H. Huxley, Darwin's Bulldog
(1825-1895)

Sketch by Th. H. Huxley, ca 1880
Eohomo riding Eohippus

It would have been laughable, had it not been so poignantly sad to see these pitiful King Knutes at this late hour enthroned in solemn state on the shore of time, bidding the great wave of scientific truth and progress to stay and come no further. Hankering after simpler times, they vainly try to force the world into biblical bounds. Unfortunately, they chose to call their procrustian product a "science." — Frank Zindler

The Dark Ages were a dismal period in history from 300 to 800 A.D. when little or nothing much (mostly nothing) happened and civilization stagnated. The beginning of the Dark Ages was synchronous with the establishment of the Christian Church. Historians agree in a direct relationship, but disagree as to whether religion was the cause or the effect of the Dark Ages.

The Book of Revelations reveals that the Gates of Heaven, which stand 12 cubits (18 feet) high, are each carved from a single pearl. The largest pearls from the oysters of Japan are about 10mm across. By upward scaling the pearls of the Gates of Heaven must have been derived from an extinct oyster the size of a football stadium. This clearly belongs in the Guiness Book of Records as the largest thing that ever lived. Larger than the biggest dinosaurs, the blue whale or the great redwood trees.

"Religious bigotry is once again abroad on the land, tilting at that old bete noire evolution" — Preston Cloud, National Academy of Sciences

2

DARWINISM

The German philosopher, Friederich Nietzsche, a century ago declared that "God is dead," a view now widely accepted. (Others hold that God is not dead but that He just doesn't want to get involved.) But who was the villain? The search by theologians quickly narrowed down to the scientists and, in turn, to Darwin and darwinism. It would seem for sure that he either killed God or left him largely unemployed. Evolution is mechanistic and explains too much rather than too little — often providing the "wrong" theological answers to the mystery of life.

Certainly it was no great cause for alarm to learn that we are related to the great apes. Other more sensitive nerve endings were touched. Evolution has an impact on every aspect of man — his metaphysics, his philosophy and his ethics. Charles Darwin, a reticent country gentleman, did not intend to stir up such a fury. His *Origin of Species* in 1859, however, was the *coup de grace* in the age-old war between science and religion. Darwin recognized that sexual reproduction creates variation in the offspring and provides more offspring than nature can expect to survive to maturity. Natural selection and survival of the fittest are the driving forces behind evolution.

Creationists would have us believe that the theory of evolution is in a state of crisis and disarray when, in fact, it is dynamic and vibrant. Argumentation among scientists, unlike religionists who defend stagnant and dogmatic positions, indicates a state of good health. Darwinism, as with all scientific theories, undergoes continuous testing and modification, but it has remained the core of modern evolutionary synthesis. One can easily find fault with the details of Darwin's classical theory but, if he were alive today, he would be the first to modify his views to account for new facts.

The purpose of science is simply to understand our world. Man, as an animal, is a part of the complete stream of life. Man and the primates, particularly the anthropoid apes, have a common ancestor. Since Darwin's time every knowing person has agreed that we are related to the apes. Nothing in nature makes sense except in the light of evolution. Christianity was responsible for the intellectual stagnation of the Dark Ages and the fundamentalist mentality of today retards our cultural and intellectual development. Fortunately, there is no way that evolution can be legislated away. It is here to stay as a monument to Darwin and to many other scientists both before and after him. For a biologist, the alternative to thinking in evolutionary terms is not to think at all.

Darwin was wrong, Man is still an ape!

All I want before I die is some assurance that the human race will be allowed to continue. --- Bertrand Russell, British Philosopher.

I know that Love is the answer, but what was the question? --- Misty Beethoven a.k.a. Bubbles Tandelaho Goldfarb.

General Percy Witherspoon of the Welsh Fusiliers had an abiding interest in ancient geneology. It comes as no surprise, then, that sharing his quarters at Down House, Surrey, was a pet chimpanzee *(Pan troglodytes)* named Darwin, a fugitive from the London Zoo. He was not the most handsome of primates; in fact, a short time earlier, he had been entered in the Ugly Animal Contest — and won! On the other hand, Darwin played chess, which Witherspoon enjoyed. And especially so because the ape was not very bright so the General invariably won.

Returning to his quarters one evening after hoisting a few at the local pub, Witherspoon was surprised, but not pleased, to find Darwin waiting up all turned out in his master's dress uniform complete with epaulettes, medals, Sam Brown belt and sword.

"You lowly cousin of Adam!" thundered the war hero, "How dare you dress out in my uniform — and up after taps, too. I should dispatch you back to the zoo."

Chagrined, Darwin put down his cigar, slowly rose and with baleful glances knuckle-walked, as is the manner of his kind, out to the hallway. Reproachfully, he shuffled back with a visiting card from Sir Julian Huxley, President of the Royal Society. The noted scientist obviously had called and, judging from an empty magnum of Mumms and an ashtray full of fine Cuban cigar ends, had been hospitably entertained. Even the chessboard was open but the pawns and pieces were scattered across the floor. Apparently Darwin once again had been checkmated — and he was a sore loser. Aware of his unfair accusation, Witherspoon apologized profusely to his progenitor and retired for the night.

As was his custom, the next evening the general ambled down to the corner pub for his usual pint of best bitter. And who should he encounter but Sir Julian nursing a snifter of brandy.

CHARLES DARWIN

"By the by, Spoon, I greatly enjoyed visiting you last evening," Sir Julian offered, "but I forgot to ask you where you got those choice cigars. Jolly good, those."

Somewhat miffed, General Witherspoon deigned not to reply but stared off into space while twirling his well-waxed mustache.

"Spoon, old boy, no offense, I was just joking," countered Sir Julian, "I knew it wasn't you before I had finished the first cigar." (Adapted from an anecdote by A. Bierce.)

To the dismay of some theologians, Darwin (1809-1882) lies buried in Westminister Abbey.

Alta: A ghost town in the Wasatch mountains of Utah recently reborn as a ski resort. Formerly a burgeoning raucus mining town of 5,000 people fueled by the discovery of silver in 1865. The presence of 6 breweries and 26 saloons did little to cool the tempers that resulted in more than 100 killings in the town's first few years.

In 1873 a stranger, claiming to be the Messiah, offered to go to the crowded little cemetery at the foot of Rustler Mountain and raise the dead. The local heirs, heiresses and remarried spouses at first were overjoyed at the prospect of this miracle but after some dispassionate consideration recognized some disadvantages to this plan. Soon the stranger left town with $2,500 raised by the concerned citizens for his traveling expenses.

Every religious cult requires a sacred story, a *mythos*, that recounts the acts of the god or goddess or gods or other sacred beings. There is really no reason to believe that Moses was anything more than a hero figure whose name has become attached to collections of ancient Hebrew law codes. Indeed, careful scholarship shows the supposed Mosaic authorship of the Pentateuch (first five books of the Old Testament) was a mosaic of authors...—Gerald Larue

3

THE NATIONAL ACADEMY OF SCIENCE SPEAKS OUT

Concerned by the threat to the integrity of science, nearly all major scientific societies have written position statements or passed resolutions opposing laws which would require the teaching of creationism. This uniform opposition applies not only to the life sciences but also to the earth and physical sciences. Even the National Academy of Science which represents science at the highest level in the U.S.A. has been prompted to publish a position paper entitled "Science and Creationism: A View from the National Academy." An extract follows:

> The National Academy of Sciences cannot remain silent. To do so would be a dereliction of our responsibility to our academic and intellectual freedom. And to the fundamental principles of scientific thought. As an historic representative of the scientific profession and designated advisor to the Federal Government in the matters of science, the Academy states unequivocally that the tenets of "Creationist Science" are not supported by scientific curriculum at any level.
>
> Still, legislators are considering, and have passed, bills that would require the introduction of biblical creationism in science classes whenever the evidence for the origin of the planet, of life, and its diverse forms, or of mankind is presented. Local school boards have passed ordinances intended to restrict the teaching of biological concepts of evolution or require what is called the "balanced treatment" of creationism and evolution. Publishers of science textbooks are under pressure to de-emphasize the accepted scientific theories of evolution while adding course material on "creation science."
>
> The teachings of creationism as advocated by and exemplified in the writings of the leading proponents of "creation science" include a problem in judgments: 1) the earth and universe are relatively young, perhaps only 6,000 to 10,000 years old; 2) the present physical form of the earth is being explained by "catastrophism", including a world-wide flood; and 3) all living things, (including humans) were created miraculously, essentially in the form we now find them. These teachings may be recognized as having been derived from the accounts of the origins in the first two chapters of Genesis in the Bible.

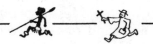

Oh what a tangled web we weave, when first we practice to deceive. --- Sir Walter Scott (1771-1832) Marmion Canto VI.

The poor may inherit the earth, but the rich will inherit the church. --- the late Bishop James A. Pike, Episcopal Church.

"CREATION SCIENCE"

In discussing their bizarre view of origins, creationists claim they are indulging in science and not religion. To test this thesis, we need only ask one question. If there were no Bible, would there be any creationists? — at least of the sort that believe in an Earth only 6,000 years old, a universal one-year flood which laid down all sedimentary strata, and a thesis which rejects evolution? The answer is obviously a resounding NO! So-called creation science exists only in the minds of Christian fundamentalists.

"Creation science" is not science since the conclusions are pre-established and are absolute and inviolate from the start. No inquiry or research is needed to discover what already has been found. The claim that creationism is valid has all the credibility of a tobacco company spokesman who denies any connection between smoking and lung cancer. Comparing this pseudo-science with real science is not like comparing apples and oranges, but more like comparing oranges and orangutangs.

Minds set in concrete:
"The Bible says it, I believe it, and that settles it."

The scientific method is an austere and spartan exercise of the brain. Any advances are slow, at best. New discoveries do not occur on a daily basis and the Eureka(!) phenomenon is rare and occurs only to the gifted few. It is no wonder that people are tempted to turn away from science and try to find some easier path to the truth — to contemplate their inner self, sit at the feet of some guru or whatever.

Creationism should be presented in biology classes in the same way that perpetual motion is presented in a thermodynamics course — as a once popular belief that was subsequently shown to be an intriguing mistake. Scientists and students are well served when a past *faux pas* is treated openly and candidly. This is an effective way to prevent students from making spectacular fools of themselves later.

The sheep will always be with us, but should they lead?

Scientific creationism is a pseudo-science similar to astrology, dianetics, Velikovskyism and pyramidology, all claiming to be scientific as this enhances their prestige and public acceptance. Yet all depend upon anti-scientific authoritarian documents, specious reasonings, supernormal occurrences, and non-mechanistic processes. All these cults repudiate any possibility of examining the relationship between cause and effect. The authentic scientific creationists have been dead for over a hundred years. Pre-Darwin creationism was the last manifestation of supernaturalism in legitimate science and was settled when Darwin organized empirical evidence for the occurrence of evolution as a realistic and materialistic process.

Creationism has been abandoned by science because it is untestable, supernaturalistic, non-mechanistic and authoritarian. To claim scientific justification for one's creationist beliefs is willful deception. Creationism has no procedure for adding new knowledge. This is of little moment to creationists for final truth has been available to them for three thousand years in the writings of Hebrew scribes of Israel. The blind acceptance of that corpus is the end to inquiry. Creationists are wedded to an inflexible pre-supposition, conclusions must precede the search for evidence whereas science is based upon skepticism and irreverence for authority. It rejects the certainty of fundamentalism.

A goalie with the Montreal Maple Leafs, a top hockey team, had a farm to which he frequently invited his team-mates. His son helped to serve large, nutritious, "meat and potatoes" meals which he derogatorily called "fodder." But one guest considered it a heavenly repast. And why not? They had the whole thing -- the fodder, the son and the goalie host.

Overheard at the Four Square Church of God Almighty in Nadir, Oklahoma: "I really don't mind Pat Robertson being born again. But did he have to come back as himself?"

5

CREATIONISM

In view of the great advances of science, it does not follow that the unknown necessarily falls into the domain of religion. Nor do we need to fabricate some interim explanation. Religious cults offer unhealthy narcissism. One is supposed to gaze inward and contemplate one's own ego as well as one's own navel to the point of hallucination. Perhaps the world's greatest religious scam is the ten percent tithe paid to the Aga Khan, a supposedly true linear descendant of Mohammed according to Shiite Moslems. The Aga Khan lives not in Iran, but in Switzerland in regal isolation from his flock.

Bible-thumpers find plenty of bogey men from "one worlders", seeking to erase national borders, to "secular humanists" which they regard as equivalent to the "fellow travelers" of the 1950's. Fundamentalists have a bushel basket of moral certainties on any subject. This is not to suppose that religion has a monoply on the ethics of morality. Preaching public morality is different from teaching public religion. The framers of the Constitution aimed to establish justice and insure domestic tranquility. As we can observe all over the world, the churches foment conflict and rebellion rather than domestic tranquility.

Creationists are guilty of gross inaccuracies, of dazzling audiences with meaningless numbers, of applying layers of confusion and gross misrepresentation. They use literature for ammunition. The game they play is find-an-arrow-in-the-wall-and-paint-a-target-around-it. One is loath to accuse Creationists of perverting ideas which they really understand, but they actually do twist ideas — as with the Second Law of Thermodynamics.

Creationists criticize orthodox science for its unsolved problems and use the problems to bolster their own model. But that only leaves the same problems unsolved. It defines them as forever unsolvable. In science, we seek data to determine what can be believed. "Creation science" seeks to buttress what has already been accepted as truth. Science seeks to understand: creationism seeks to confirm belief. Science offers proof without certainty, religion offers certainty without proof.

Creationism has not been altered or revised since the Book of Genesis was written by early Jewish prophets and primitive tribesmen about 3,000 years ago. Those who cavalierly reject the theory of evolution as not adequately supported by facts seem to forget that their own model is supported by no facts at all. Evolution forms the warp and woof of modern biology, its very fabric.

Creationists are pitted against all the Nobel Prize winners alive today, against every scientific society, and against the accumulated knowledge of the ages. These believers in biblical inerrancy have declared their anti-science judgment against all evidence of science: astronomy...wrong!, biology...guilty!, and geology...a fraud! Creationists also reject Einsteinian physics as a false doctrine that leads straight to moral laxity, or so they think.

Among fundamentalists, conclusions precede the search for evidence. They are wedded to biblical inerrancy and hyperliteral reading of the Scripture. In a time when science has cracked the genetic code and discovered the detailed mechanism of evolution within the framework of the DNA molecule, the effort of creationists to turn back the clock has a certain dream-like quality.

Scientific creationism is simply the latest attempt of the fundamentalists to sneak their sectarian myths into the public schools — to bring Sunday school into Monday school. Creationism has all the characteristics of pseudo-science. It starts with answers and searches for questions. It studies only ancient writings, it performs no experiments and makes no inquiry of nature. Creationism, like other pseudo-sciences, is indifferent to facts, tolerates erroneous calculations, ignores conflicting empirical evidence, uses faulty logic and incoherent arguments to reach conclusions. Creationists have the attitude of "whatever feels good, believe it", and they go to the public with their claim rather than to the professional community.

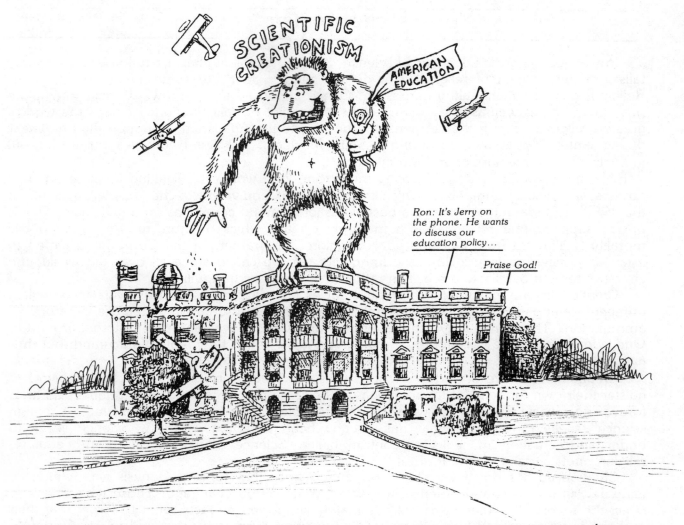

Many scientists accept evolution but are also devoutly religious. A great many religious leaders accept evolution on scientific grounds without relinquishing their belief in religious principles. Both groups regard it as false to think that the theory of evolution represents an irreconcilable conflict between religion and science. Others say that religion and science need not contradict one another, but can co-exist without intruding into each other's realm. Another view is that religion and science are separate and mutually exclusive realms of human thought whose presentation in the same context leads to misunderstanding of both scientific and religious beliefs. No doubt, this is a useful strategy to give evolution respectability in the eyes of non-scientists. But it seems a pity that this is regarded as necessary, because evolution is an established scientific theory in its own right. Trying to reconcile evolution and religion inevitably leads to "double think". Orwell defines double think as "the power of holding two contradictory beliefs in one's mind simultaneously and accepting both of them".

What if the creationists prevail? They might. By one estimate there are 75 million of their kind in the U.S. who choose the Bible and reject science, preferring faith to evidence. There is the pervasive uneasiness and a fear of science which caters to fundamentalism. For one thing, science is tentative and its theories are subject to revision. Mathematical language is arcane and understood by a very few and the vistas it offers are often frightening. This is disillusioning to the uneducated who turn to the rigid certainty of the Bible instead. There is something comforting about a view that permits no deviation and spares the painful necessity of thinking.

Creationism is not a science but a form of anti-science whose more vocal practitioners, despite their Master's and Doctor's degrees in sciences, play fast and loose with the facts of geology and biology. "Creation science" cannot exist independently of the Bible. The ultimate test of the scientist is whether one publishes research papers in the standard refereed scientific journals of which there are more than 3,000. Among the creationist scientists who took part in the Arkansas trial, only one could be identified who ever published even a single such paper.

Creationist hucksters sell a product they can neither display nor verify. Their religion indicates an unsoundness of mind and a psychotic inability to accept reality. In our egalitarian society, there should be no "chosen people". Their preachers speak of "gospel truth" avoiding the need to present any evidence. The scientists do not say, "I believe," but "I think."

Is creationism dangerous or just amusing? It is dangerous because fundamentalists, by their organized voting block, may impose their bizarre ideas upon the rest of us. James Watt, former Secretary of the Interior and a fundamentalist, testifying concerning the opening up of government lands for mineral exploitation, entered a disturbing statement in the Congressional Record. He said there was no need to conserve our natural resources because there will be a Second Coming of the Messiah in the near future. What's wrong? Watt's wrong!!

Much of religion is not relevant to modern life. Take, for example, the Tenth Commandment. Not many of us have neighbors with a maid servant, an ox or an ass which we can covet.

I know that a community of God-seekers is a great shelter for mankind. But when this grows into an institution it gives ready access to the Devil by the backdoor. --- Rabindranath Tagore, Indian Philosopher.

In her book on Christian Science, *Science and Health: Key to the Scriptures*, Mary Baker Eddy wrote in a style which is totally unintelligible. It is traced in a style often delightfully poetic but sometimes syntactically overly complex and often obscurely metaphorical. She was extremely aware of the importance of vivid, interesting terminology, including the coining of new terms. This has been taken as prima facie evidence for profundity. Before deceiving others, she succeeded in deceiving herself. She would have been well advised to follow the advice of E.B. White who said, "Be obscure clearly."

"It is impossible to travel faster than the speed of light, and certainly not desirable, as one's hat keeps blowing off." — Steve Allen.

Those who cannot remember the past are condemned to repeat it. — George Santayana

The intellectuals find religion false, the masses find it true, governments find it useful.

It is not equal time that creationists want; it is silence.

Dealing with religious zealots is one of the prudent citizen's survival skills, and we have forgotten it.

6

THE CREATIONIST'S CREED

Swearing to a creed, a dogma or any rigid set of beliefs is an anathema to scientists. How can one objectively do research when the conclusions are already fore-ordained? Scientists study Nature to learn *what is*, not *what should be*. They do not search for or expect moral messages in Nature as she is neither moral nor immoral but simply amoral.

Scientists are under no compulsion to force their findings to agree with the Bible, the Koran, or the Egyptian Book of the Dead. In contrast, nearly all the "high priests" of creationism are members of the Creation Research Society headquartered in Ann Arbor, Michigan. By swearing to a creed as a condition for membership, creationists forfeit any right to claim being scientific. An extract from their creed follows:

> All members...must subscribe to the following...the Bible is the written word of God, and because we believe it to be inspired throughout, all of its assertations are historically and scientifically true in all of the original autographs. To the student of nature, this means that the account of the origins of Genesis is a factual presentation of simple historical truth...all basic types of living things, including man, were made by direct creative acts of God during Creation Week...the Noachian Deluge, was an historical event, worldwide in its extent and effect.

The differences between the standard creation model and the usual biblical teachings are so minute that nobody's kidding anybody and nobody's being fooled. Once one hears the creation scheme spelled out, he will recognize it immediately as the Genesis model unless one was born an Australian aborigine and never heard of the Bible. One must conclude that so-called "scientific creationism" is nothing more than a religious scheme to invade the public schools with religion and a system of apologetics for the literal interpretation of Genesis. The creationist literature is written not for scientists, but for church audiences.

Creation is essentially a religious faith. Why deny it? Why hide it? Why try to sneak religion into the public schools as sort of a Trojan horse? A chorus of the opponents of the Two Model approach holds that there is a distinction between what they call scientific creationism and special creation; that the idea of a creator is not necessarily out of the Bible; and that the idea of a great catastrophe is not necessarily biblical. But this isn't fooling anybody. The real issue is the battle of creationism versus evolution. And everybody knows it. — Richard G. Elmendorf, noted creationist and unrepentent geocentrist.

Having completed his usual sermon on air, wind and smoke, the text taken from the *Book of Macadamia*, the good pastor intoned, "Now let us all rise and sing hymn No. 603, "Lead On, O Kinky Turtle." At that, the parishoners fell to mumbling and stirring. The reverend then closed his eyes and shook his head saying, "Sorry, that was the choir boys name for it." Recovering both his composure and solemnity, he once again instructed the parishoners to stand and "sing hymn number 603, Lead On, O King Eternal."

7

PLATE TECTONICS CREED

As professional skeptics, scientists are amused by creeds as science remains ever a fluid search for the truth — a goal sometimes approached but *never fully attained*. A decade or so ago, *plate tectonics* (more popularly known as *continental drift*) became a consensus view as to how the world works geologically. There is little doubt but that plate tectonics is a true model for terrestrial tectonism. But in an effort to keep it from becoming a dogma, a creed (with apologies to the Nicean Creed) has been satirically devised.

"I believe in Plate Tectonics Almighty, Unifier of the Earth Sciences, and explanation of all things geological and geophysical; and in our Xavier LaPichon, revealer of relative motion, deduced from spreading rates about all ridges; Hypotheses of Hypothesis, Theory of Theory, Very Fact of Very Fact; deduced not assumed; Continents of being of one unit with the Oceans, from which all plates spread; Which, when they encounter another plate and are subducted, go down in Benioff Zones, and are resorbed into the Aesthenosphere, and are made Mantle; and cause earthquake foci also under Island Arcs; They soften and can flow; and at the Ridges magma rises again according to Vine and Matthews; and ascends into the Crust, and maketh symmetrical magnetic anomalies; and the sea floor shall spread again, with continents, to make both mountains and faults, Whose evolution shall have no end.

And I believe in Continental Drift, the Controller of the evolution of Life, Which proceedeth from Plate Tectonics and Sea-Floor Spreading; Which with Plate Tectonics and Sea-Floor Spreading together is worshipped and glorified; Which was spake of by Wegener; and I believe in one Seismic and Volcanistic pattern; I acknowledge one Cause for the deformation of rocks, And I patiently look for the eruption of new Ridges and the subduction of the Plates to come. Amen." (from Scharnberger and Kern, 1972)

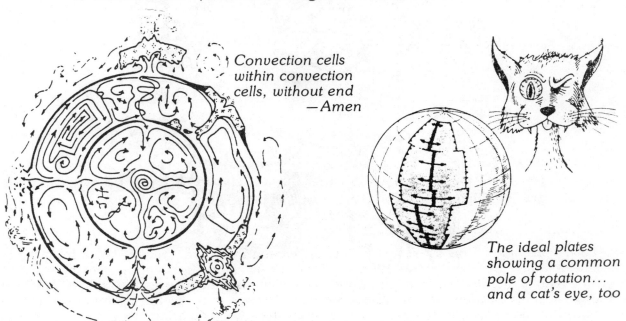

Convection cells within convection cells, without end —Amen

The ideal plates showing a common pole of rotation... and a cat's eye, too

8

EQUAL TIME

The fact that some people earnestly believe in special creation is insufficient to make it a subject within the framework of science. It is a legitimate matter to discuss this belief in a course in history, sociology, philosophy or psychology. Creation science is Orwellian "newspeak", trading on the prestige of science. It is easy to be impressed by something one doesn't understand. Their effort is to control thought rather than to understand nature.

To think clearly and freely is the best defense against tyranny. If we wish our schools to remain free and open to complex ideas we will have to fight to see that they remain so. After putting a man on the moon, there is still a substantial contingent of people who believe that the earth was created in 6 days, 6,000 years ago, and is flat.

Equal time for creation and evolution in public schools would allow proponents of such pseudo-sciences as astrology, pyramidology, ancient astronauts and revisionist history to overstep the professional rules of peer review and use political pressure to legislate their way into our educational system. School curricula would not be in the hands of scientists and educators, but would be determined by politicians swaying in the winds of ideologic religious pressure groups.

The creationists' appeal for equal time in the public schools is simply the smile of the crocodile. Once they have their foot in education's door they want all the time there is. It would be like giving equal time to astrology in an astronomy class or to phrenology in a course in psychology.

Equal time: Monday school in Sunday school.

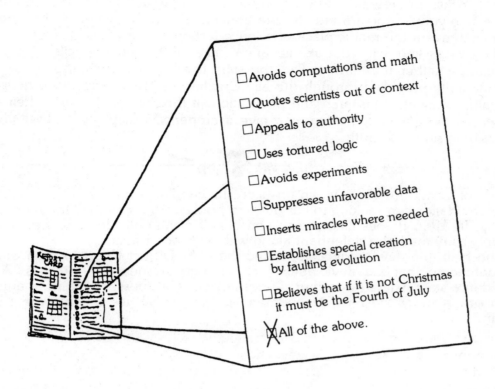

Creationists' Report Card

The image shows a checklist with the following items:
- Avoids computations and math
- Quotes scientists out of context
- Appeals to authority
- Uses tortured logic
- Avoids experiments
- Suppresses unfavorable data
- Inserts miracles where needed
- Establishes special creation by faulting evolution
- Believes that if it is not Christmas it must be the Fourth of July
- All of the above. (checked)

While there cannot be the slightest objection to teaching Genesis in our public schools as a creation myth, among others of a similar kind, in courses, say, on anthroplogy, it is the sheerest humbug to claim that such stories have anything to do with science. Creationists refer to their manipulations as "creation science", but they are no more scientific than Christian Science or Scientology. A science is characterized neither by a willingness to believe or to disbelieve, nor wish to disprove anything, but a desire to discover *what is* and to do so by observation, experimentation, and verification. No scientist can be a fundamentalist in his attitude toward truth. They do not believe in fundamental and absolute certainties. Science also does not deal in miracles. Apples might start to rise tomorrow or drift sideways but the possibility does not merit equal time in the science classroom.

In recent years there has been a push by creationists to pass laws requiring the teaching of creationism in science classes whenever evolution is taught. The intent is not so much to teach creationism, with which children have already been thoroughly indoctrinated in Sunday school, but to silence any mention of evolution. Equal time laws have been struck down by federal courts in Arkansas and Louisiana as being in violation of the separation of church and state clause of the First Amendment. Although "creation science" advocates contend that creationism is a science, the courts disagree. They concur with the scientific community that creationism is religion and *not* science. The struggle continues, but now mainly at the school board level.

The creationists in the battle to legislate biblical creationism into the schools like to claim that atheism is also a religion — and which they say is already being taught in violation of the First Amendment. Atheism is *not* a religion but the lack thereof. Atheists have neither a liturgy, ceremony, ritual, revelations, dogma, miracles, clergy nor a deity — and atheism is not based on faith and is not a course offered in school.

As Edward Erickson notes, the basic objection to giving equal time to creation "science" in the classroom revolves not around its questionable merit. Rather it is the attempt by creationists to circumvent the marketplace of science testing with a political solution. Modern society should be finished with the medieval practice of having councils of bishops or parliaments ruling whether the earth is flat, the stars fixed, illnesses caused by demons or witches supernaturally propelled through the air. Creationists are free to make their case in the give and take of scientific research and publication. If their views are valid, their doctrine will survive on its merit. If not, no law can give it credence except by authoritarians who confuse political coersion with truth.

Ralph Forbes of London, Arkansas, an unsuccessful candidate for the U.S. Senate, filed a lawsuit just before Halloween seeking to bar public schools from observing "the rites of Satan" on that holiday. In 1986 Forbes filed the suit on behalf of himself, Jesus Christ, and minor children. Satan was named as a defendant along with a school district.

Lawyer John Hall, the devil's advocate, asked the U.S. District Court to drop Satan as a defendant, contending that the devil doesn't do enough business in Arkansas. A person cannot be sued in a state where he neither resides nor does business. Hall further argued that dismissal is in order under the First Amendment as the suit alleges a controversy between Jesus Christ and Satan.

Representative James Cooper (R. Mesa, Az.), a Mormon, has five times introduced unsuccessful legislation in Arizona which would have required the teaching of creationism on a par with evolution. On one occasion the law passed both houses but was vetoed by the governor. (Cartoon by Benson, Arizona Republic, reprinted by permission.)

9

BIBLE INERRANCY AND INFALLIBILITY

To accept the hyperliteral interpretation of the Bible one must assume that ancient writers (unlike their modern counterparts) never lied, never exaggerated, and never indulged the truth. One must also assume that nothing is lost in the translation of ancient Hebrew to modern English. This would seem to be a departure from human nature, more striking than the departure from the laws of physics and chemistry required by the biblical miracles.

No one has ever claimed that the Bible is *totally* in error. Virtually any book available on a library shelf has some truth therein. The question is one of degree and not kind. However, the Bible is permeated with error and cannot reasonably be regarded as inerrant. Fundamentalists raise the Bible to the status of a "Paper Pope". By this device, they have a perfect sanctuary to which they can retreat with impunity whenever engaged in controversy. It is said that the Devil quotes Scripture to suit his purpose.

A Renaissance literature class in an eastern university was assigned the task of translating the 23rd Psalm from English to French, then to Spanish, and back to English. The final product revealed, not unsurprisingly that much is lost in any translation. The new version reads: God is my guide, but I don't want. He brings me down in grassy fields. He brings out my spirits, and leads me to waters. He sends me the right way: His way". etc. etc. Imagine what has happened from early sacred writing in Hebrew, through Greek, to old English...to now.

The conflict between science and the Bible has been fired anew recently because of the struggle between evolution and creationism. The battles are being fought at many sites — the schools, libraries, and courts. The unscientific nature of the Bible is revealed by many mythological creatures being spoken of as if they were real. Some of the more prominent examples are cockatrices, unicorns, satyrs and fiery serpents. Hundreds of miracles are contained within the Scripture and these more than anything else prove that the book is not scientifically valid. Miracles by definition are supernatural and science by definition does not accept the supernatural. Any book claiming a woman turned into a pillar of salt, the sun turned backward ten degrees on the sundial, and whales came out of the sea can hardly be classed as scientific. Logic, reasoning and skepticism accompany a scientific mentality rather than faith and uncritical belief.

The debate on biblical inerrancy has been aired in academic circles for centuries with liberals viewing conservatives as hopelessly unscholarly and conservatives accusing liberals of undermining the inspiration and authority of the Bible. There has always been a debate on the inerrancy of the Word, usually based on theological rather than literary grounds. But this argumentation has been expressed with a shrillness that made it impossible for most scholars to take seriously.

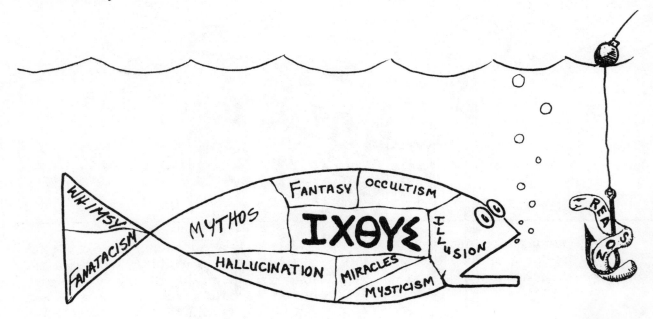

HOLY MACKEREL !

Those believing the Bible to be scientifically inerrant, precise and wise beyond its years should be aware of the following biblical assertions: (a) The bat is not a flying mammal, but a bird (Lev. 11:13, 19, Deut. 14:11, 18); (b) Some fowls have four feet (Lev. 11:20-21); (c) Some creeping insects have only four legs (Lev. 11:23, 42); (d) Camels do not have cloven-hooves (Lev. 11:4)½ (e) The earth was formed out of water (2 Peter 3:5); (f) The earth rests on pillars (1 Sam. 2:8); (g) The earth does not move, but stands still (1 Chron. 16:30); (h) The rainbow is not as old as rain and sunshine (Gen. 9:13); (i) A mustard seed is the smallest of all seeds and grows in the greatest of all plants (Matt. 13:31-32); (j) Turtles have voices (Song of Sol. 2:12); (k) The earth has ends and edges (Job 37:3); (l) The earth has four corners (Isa. 11:12, Rev. 7:1); (m) Some four-legged animals fly (Lev. 11:21); (n) The world's languages didn't evolve slowly but appeared suddenly (Gen. 112:6-9); and (o) A fetus can understand speech (Luke 1:44).

The Skeptic

"If God permits such misery to exist, He cannot be good, and if He is powerless to prevent it, he cannot be God."
—*Buddha*

"In religion what damned error but some somber brow will bless it, and approve it with a text."
—*Shakespeare*

"I count religion but a childish toy, And hold there is no sin but ignorance."
—*Christopher Marlow*
from *The Jew of Malta*

"Scratch a Christian and you find a pagan — spoiled."
—*Israel Zangwill*

"And that's the way it is..."
—*Walter Cronkite*

"Religion is an attempt to get control over the sensory world, in which we are placed, by means of the wish-world, which we have developed inside us as a result of biological and psychological necessities."
—*Sigmund Freud*

Salvation is not begged or bought;
Too long this selfish hope sufficed;
Too long man reeked with lawless thought;
And leaned upon a tortured Christ.
—*Ella Wheeler Wilcox*

"The time will come when our posterity will wonder at our ignorance of things so plain."
—*Seneca*

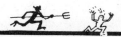

10

ST. AUGUSTINE AND BIBLE INERRANCY

In the 5th century A.D., St. Augustine offered some thoughts concerning biblical errancy. He wrote the following in his treatise, *On the Literal Meaning of Genesis:* "In points that are obscure, or far from clear, if we should read anything into the Bible that may allow of several instructions consistently with the faith to be taught, let us not commit ourselves to any of these with such precipitous obstinacy that when, perhaps, the truth is more diligently searched into, this may fall to the ground, and we with it...It often falls out that a Christian may not fully understand some point about the earth, the sky or the distance of the stars; the known vagaries of the sun and the moon; the circuits of years and epochs, the nature of animals, fruits, stones, and other things of that sort, and hence may not expound it rightly or make it clear by experiences. Now it is too absurd, ay!, most pernicious and to be avoided at all costs, for an infidel to find a Christian so stupid as to argue these matters as if they were Christian doctrine; he will be unable to contain his laughter at seeing error written in the skies."

At the Catholic Inquisition in 1610, Galileo frequently quoted St. Augustine when defending himself against the charges of infidelity to the Bible. He was forced to recant his belief that the earth moves and revolves around the Sun. But when leaving the courtroom Galileo muttered, *"Eppur si muove."* (But still it moves.")

JERRY FALWELL: PROPHET OF PROFIT (NEWS ITEM)

The Moral Majority can't make political contributions, but the affiliated *I Love America Committee* can. Falwell is president of both non-profit corporations, and the committee is administered from Moral Majority's downtown headquarters. The *I Love America Committee* raised $485,000 in its first year, but spent $413,000 raising it and owed $38,000 more to various suppliers at the end of the latest reporting period.

The committee gave $43,000 directly to candidates and $11,000 to other political groups

during the year. Some of the donations were in the form of in-kind contributions of printing or postage. Much of the help went to unsuccessful candidates. For example, $1,000 was given to the born-again former Black Panther leader Eldridge Cleaver, who was planning to run against Rep. Ronald Dellums, D-CA. Cleaver dropped out of the race before the primary. Two unsuccessful candidates for local Lynchburg offices got almost a quarter of the money given to candidates. Harry Covert, a former member of the Moral Majority staff, got $3,000 for his 1983 Senate race. Chauncy Spencer's campaign for Lynchburg City Council received $7,000, the largest donation made by the group. The most generous donation reported was apparently unknown to the recipient. The $7,000 allotted to Spencer was given instead on April 24 to Calvin Falwell, Jerry Falwell's cousin. But the report said it was for Spencer, an independent.

The *I Love America Committee* has relied heavily on **direct-mail** solicitations offering donors several gifts in exchange for $120 in annual dues. The purpose of the committee, according to its mailings, is to get conservative candidates "who will support the Judeo-Christian tradition" elected to office.

If the liberals win in November, says one recent mailing, "you might as well put your Bible under the mattress, fold up your American flags and throw away all your coins that say 'In God We Trust'."

The Rise and Fall of Man

In Orange County, California one woman gave her $40,000 home to the World Wide Church of God. She was then immediately eligible as a public charge to enter a convalescent home. The bill picked up by MediCal and MediCare ran to $700.00 per month, more than her social security income. A Los Angeles Times headline said it all: "Church Gets Her Home, Public Her Bills".

The first rule of good health is to have only those diseases you can afford. And the first rule of an acceptable religion is to believe only in those things you would like to: e.g., life after death or reincarnaton.

12

"I SAW JESUS IN A TORTILLA" (NEWS ITEM)

A few years ago Ramona Barreras saw what she says is the face of Jesus in a tortilla she baked. So Mrs. Barreras said she asked Jesus, "Lord, if this is from you I need some confirmation." She said the letter "J" then appeared on the face. Then a Mexican weekly, El Sol, published an article about this apparition. Since then the tortilla has been preserved in shellac, swaddled in a purple shawl and kept in a box for viewing. She plans to write the Guiness Book of World Records, as well as the 700 Club, a syndicated Christian program that recounts the stories of those who have witnessed miracles. She is also thinking about a movie. But she says her tortilla is not for profit, but to share. "I think it's just an open door to faith," she says. (News item)

BORN AGAIN? Many people claim to be born-again Christians, but this is nonsense. Children are born free of religion and the concept of God is an indoctrination. A person cannot deny his genetic makeup such as his race — being of Irish or German extraction. Religion is not passed on from generation to generation through the genes. It is acquired environmentally, so a person cannot be born-again, but only a re-indoctrinated Christian. Religion is a matter of personal choice and can be disavowed at any time. A child is not born with a crucifix around his neck or the Star of David stamped on his arm. (Uncle Thaddeus had an eight-ball tattooed on his forehead, but he was a throw-back.) According to Israeli law, anyone with a Jewish mother is Jewish — the determination is matrilineal. According to Hitler any person with at least one Jewish grandparent was defined as Jewish. (He also claimed with contorted logic, that the Jews were a nation, rather than just a religion because they had not signed the Geneva Convention. Hitler argued that Jewish prisoners were not protected by its provisions.)

Classical paranoia and paranoid schizophrenia have been blamed for producing cults. A person who founds a cult asserts the arrogant claim that he (above all others) has achieved a miraculous cultural breakthrough, a claim that outsiders may perceive as a delusion of grandeur. For example, L. Ron Hubbard in 1950 announced his invention of Dianetics (later to become Scientology) by saying that "the creation of dianetics is a milestone for Man comparable to his discovery of fire and superior to his inventions of the wheel and arch". --- W. Bainbridge and R. Stork in *Religion and Religiosity in America*.

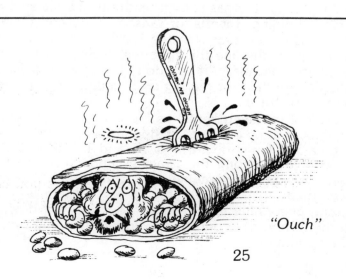

"Ouch"

?Como frijoles?
(How have you bean?)

25

13

ORAL ROBERTS: CLOSE ENCOUNTERS OF THE HALLUCINATORY KIND
(NEWS ITEM)

In 1983, in a bold religious fund raising appeal, evangelist Oral Roberts sent out millions of letters saying that Jesus appeared and told him that God had chosen Roberts to find the cure for cancer. Roberts said that the Lord told him to ask his hundreds of thousands of "prayer partners" to send him $240 each to complete the Tower of Faith Research Center in Tulsa, Oklahoma, where the cure for cancer would be discovered. Roberts, saying that cancer is the work of Satan, appealed for donations on the basis of what he described as a seven-hour conversation between Jesus and himself.

Roberts claimed two years ago that he had a vision of a 900-foot tall Jesus. This alleged apparition generated millions of dollars in donations for his City of Faith Medical Center in Tulsa. This 60-story diagnostic clinic and 30-story hospital were opened in 1981 after an extended battle with Oklahoma State Health authorities who said that the city already had a surplus of hospital facilities. Roberts fund-raising letter drew sharp criticism from individuals and from Colorado Governor Richard Lamm's Citizen Advocate Office which accused Roberts of using unfair pressure to solicit money from elderly widows.

Later in 1983, in a twelve-page letter of appeal, Roberts described his orders from the Lord. He quoted the Lord as telling him: "...I am going to bring mighty and great breakthroughs for the cure of cancer...but are you and your prayer partners going to obey me? And when?"

Marilyn Russom of Bartlesville, Oklahoma, a cancer victim, received a copy of Roberts' appeal letter and complained that she was "deeply disturbed by Roberts' attempt to capitalize on fears of those of us who are faced with a terminal disease. In my judgment it is both immoral and un-Christian for this TV con-man to divert badly needed research dollars from research centers, like Sloan-Kettering and Stanford University." While acknowledging that he is not a scientist or medical researcher, Roberts told his prospective donors that he had learned by divine insight that cancer is a spiritual disorder as well as a physical disease. He wrote: "This is not Oral Roberts asking you for $240, but the Lord."

Being a big-time televangelist is not a piece of cake these days. Witness the plight of Oral Roberts, the funamentalist from Tulsa, Oklahoma. Citing yet another financial crisis at his Faith Medical Center, Roberts warned his "sheep" in January of 1987 that if he doesn't get $4,500,000 in "quick money", God is not going to let him live past March. In other words, "Send me money or I die." Ouch! Of course, Roberts couched this divine threat in terms dripping with pretentious piety. He has shown us the unseemly side of the Almighty. God is an extortionist and He is holding Roberts for ransom. God and Oral Roberts are (or at least were) old pals and he has gotten oral with the Lord some 30 different times over the past years. But God has laid it on the line this time telling Roberts he has got to raise some big bucks to support his ministry because, "If you don't I am going to call you home." Now being "called home" is actually God-talk for the big chill, getting croaked, bumped off, zapped, or terminated with extreme prejudice.

God's threats should not be taken lightly as He is one tough cookie. Just read *all* of the Bible not just those namby-pamby excerpts cited in church — and especially read the *Book of Numbers:* "Soon a great, sullen mob formed ... and the awsome glory of the Lord was seen." God's anger went out among the Israelites and He unleashed a plague that killed 14,700. "And that was with Moses pleading with Him to take it easy! And, elsewhere ... a great fissure swallowed them up, along with their tents and families and the friends who were standing with them, and everything they owned. So they went down alive into Hell and the earth closed around them, and they perished." Now if that is not enough to rot your socks, read on in the Old Testament.

Reprinted with permission of the Phoenix Gazette

Rev. Twiddle Dee: "Holy Guacamole! Here's a news item about a school system that doesn't pervert children's minds with philosophy, literature, social studies, the arts, history, and the rest of that secular humanist bunk!"
Rev. Twiddle Dum: "Halleluja! Holy Toledo! Where is it?"
Rev. Twiddle Dee: "Russia."

Where the Bible and Truth are found to conflict, the atheist says the Bible should be discarded; the liberal atheist says the interpretation must be revised; but the fundamentalist says the truth is a lie.

If faith is separated from fact, it is only another form of what we call today a "trip".

Gee! Oral, just think what I could do if I had your kind of money!

SNAPPY DRESSER, TOO...

HOLDEN 86

It's a simple matter of the quick or the dead. Quick money or a dead Oral Roberts. One can visualize thousands of little old ladies endorsing their social security checks over to his ministry rather than have his demise in their heads. It seems unlikely that God wants Oral Roberts dead. As the Mafia has long known, dead clients are slow in paying their debts. Just when it appeared that the country had seen virtually every type of money-grubbing gimmick, Roberts came up with a new twist...the ultimate threat. Surely the patron saint of Oral Roberts' ministry is P.T. Barnum. Happily, as David Brinkley reported in January 1987 on his weekly news show, "Oral Roberts is still with us … But stay tuned."

Actually, through one simple gesture, Roberts could have converted millions of agnostics and atheists to Christianity. As Mike Royko of the Chicago Tribune pointed out, all he had to do was drop dead on March 31, 1987. He could have been zapped by a big lightning stroke while on TV in front of millions, leaving behind only a smoking pair of empty shoes. There would have been no cause for sorrow as Roberts had a personalized guarantee to enter the gates of heaven. Just think of the impact his prophesized demise would have had on the Soviet Union. No need for Star Wars when God is on our side.

CREATIONISM VERSUS EVOLUTION
As Taught In Texas Public Schools

Adam and Eve, and Cain and Abel
Were sitting around the dinner table
When little Abel began to grouse:
"Why don't we ever go to grandma's house?"

    Little did little Abel know
    That he had no grandmother, even though
    Subsequent people, like me and you
    Would have not one grandmother, but two.

        So Eve and Adam had to explain
        The facts of life to Abel and Cain;
        Eve, putting Abel in his crib
        Told how she'd come from Adam's rib.

Then Adam told the boys his story:
How he'd been made in a blaze of glory,
And then how Eve had been created
And how, on their first date, they'd mated.

    "That's how you boys were born," he said,
    "So now, before you go to bed
    "You know it takes both man and wife
    "To join to make new human life."

        "If that's the case it's pretty plain
        "We'll both need girl-friends," muttered Cain,
        "But until Eve again gives birth
        "We two are the only kids on earth!"

So Eve told Adam: 'Let's try, and maybe
"We can create a female baby.
"Then Cain and Abel can do the rest
"Even though it'll be incest!"

    A girl was born. Thanks to a brother
    She soon became the second mother.
    Then further births followed apace
    As they begat the human race.

        Yes, that's the story of creation
        Accepted without hesitation
        'Til Darwin claimed we came from apes
        Who evolved to our present shapes.

    Did Adam or Orang-utan
    Father the race of modern man?
    The chances are we'll never know —
    It happened many years ago.

14

Agnostic: A gutless atheist.

Chicken Cacciatore: An early convert to Christianity who in 64 A.D. chose not to be martyred in Rome's coliseum.

Christianity: One of several only true religions achieved not by coming to the faith at the end of a long journey but by standing still. Christians become so by a lucky accident of birth—being born in the right place. Otherwise, Heaven forbid!, one might end up a Muslim, a Jew, or a Sikh. To be a member of the correct sub-set of Christianity, say Catholicism, one must choose his parents wisely. One does not need to embrace a religion as it embraces you. All this obviates choice, evaluation, and independent inquiry.

Faith: A belief in something known to be false.

Heaven: Never-never Land adjacent to the Void, formerly thought to be in the sky just beyond the Firmament. Modern space research has made this location dubious so that Heaven is not regarded as being far beyond Nowhere.

Hebrew: A male Jew as opposed to a She-brew...A. Bierce.

Hymnal: A liturgical songbook for use in a church, cathedral, basilica, synagogue, masjid, oratory, chantry, or sacarium where words too bizarre, fanciful, or whimsical to be recited aloud may yet be sung with perfect propriety.

Auditorium: An indoor gathering place where evangelists of the electronic media pack their paid audiences to, on cue, nod in agreement, look evangelical, or exclaim Hallelujah! Much is spoken at great length and with firm conviction, but little is said. Yet as the Reverend Norman Vincent Glockenspiel has so aptly remarked, "Bad breath is better than no breath at all." Being a family enterprise, the evangelist is generally accompanied by his wife, mother-in-law, son, and other miscellaneous progeny who attest to his devotion to family, motherhood, and the U.S. (Semper 'Fi') Marines. Etymologically, the word *auditorium* has mixed roots. *Audio* derives from the Greek — *to hear*. *Toro* comes from the Spanish meaning "bull."

LLD: An honorary degree granted to superstars of the electronic pulpit who collect more than $50,000,000 per annum; for example, Jerry Falwell, Oral Roberts, Jimmy Swaggart, and Pat Robertson. Originally derived from the British currency usage LLd. (Or in American terminology $$¢.) To encourage a silent collection, without the disturbing tinkle of coins, the *d* is now commonly dropped.

Moonies: Followers of a latter day messiah, the Reverend Sun Myung Moon of the Unification Church, a late entry into the Religion of the Month Club. Maharishis of this cult skillfully combine the worship of mammon, moolah, and mysticism. Moonies are not to be confused with the curry-scented Hare Krishnas with their saffron robes, thongs, tambourines, and Kojak haircuts. Rev. Moon offers the best in false messiah-ship, heresy, and counterfeit theology.

Papal bull: Papal bull.

Paranormal: Included under this rubric are: Mesmerism, Clairvoyance, E.S.P., U.F.O. apparitions, Loch Ness monsters, telepathy, psychokinesis, poltergeists, exorcisms,

Life, liberty, and the happiness of pursuit

The first divine was the first rogue who met the first fool.---Voltaire (1694-1778)

We have just enough religion to make us hate, but not enough to make us love one another. —*Jonathon Swift, 1706*

I find it remarkable that Eve was in no way surprised to hear a snake talk.

How does it happen that so many people with a comparatively high level of intelligence cannot distinguish between fantasy and reality? --- Z. Zed Zyzyx

---

An atheist is a person with no invisible means of support. --- Bishop Fulton J. Sheen

---

A day without religion is a day of sunshine. --- John Frank McHone, Soldier of Fortune, a misfortune.

Creationism is wrong! Totally and absolutely wrong. In the degrees of wrongness, creationism is at the top of the scale. Creationists pull every trick to justify their position. They verge right over into the downright bizarre. Scientific creationism is not only wrong, it is ludicrous. It is a grotesque parody of human thought, and is a downright misuse of human intelligence. To the believer, it is an insult to God. --- Michael Ruse: in *Darwin Defended*.

Many good men believed the strange fables of Christianity and have lived very good lives — for credulity is not a crime.

reincarnations, Bermuda Triangles, biblical prophecies, levitation, horoscopes, and Christian Science healings. In short something rarely, if ever seen — like horse manure in a garage.

Piety: Reverence for the Supreme Being based upon his supposed resemblance to man.

Primate: (1) the head of a church. In the Anglican Church (The Church of England) there are two primates — the Archbishop of York, who is a Primate of England, and the Archbishop of Cantebury, who is the Primate of All England. (2) Any of an order of higher mammals, including the lemurs, tarsiers, monkeys, gibbons, great apes, and Man — and both the archbishops of York and Canterbury.

Rationalization: A method of logic whereby creationists reach conclusions of their choice by mixing perplexity with complexity and sprinkling in the spice of conscious mendacity so as to avoid painful revelation.

Reality: A myth shared by a large number of people. "Convince enough people of a lie and it becomes the truth" — Rev. Phinaeus Crabtree, 1874.

Revelation: (1) The final book of the Holy Writ, commonly ascribed to the apostle John, but by others to Baron Munchausen or the brothers Grimm. (2) A biblical book of riddles which requires for its understanding a revelation. (3) The last of some 66 books of the Bible in which St. John the Divine concealed all that he knew. The prophecies and wisdom of the prophets are divulged in full disagreement.

Sabbath: Sunday, the Holy Day of Rest. Except, if you are a Jew, then Saturday. Except if you are Muslim, then Friday. Except if you are a Sikh, then Thursday. Except for Uncle Thaddeus, who rests every day including Sundays.

"Why doesn't he try praying?"

PART 2
CREATIONISM AND FUNDAMENTALISM

Moses, the tame raven, was a spy and a tale-bearer, but he was also a clever talker. He claimed to know of a mysterious country called Sugar Candy Mountain where all animals went when they died. It was situated somewhere up in the sky, a little distance beyond the clouds. At Sugar Candy Mountain, it was Sunday seven days a week, clover was in season all year round, and lump sugar and linseed cake grew on hedges. The other animals hated Moses because he told tales and did no work, but some of them believed in Sugar Candy Mountain, and the pigs had to argue very hard to persuade them that there was no such place. --- George Orwell, *Animal Farm*

Creationists are guilty of an unholy trinity — they misrepresent scientific theories and scientists' motives; they suppress relevent evidence; and they unhesitantly fabricate imaginary facts to support creationism. They are to be condemned for their blatant disrespect for the truth. --- A. Aaron Aardvark.

It is doubtful that even the most ardent fundamentalist really accepts the Bible as wholly inerrant. There are at least three theological disciplines which attempt to straighten the Bible out — *hermaneutics*, *exegesis*, and *apologetics*. The result is Dalmation theology which, like the firehouse dog, is spotty.

1

FUNDAMENTALISM

Fundamentalism is a religion, not Religion. Zealots espouse a position which is not the normative posture of Christianity. Fundamentalists accept the origin of the Earth and Man as described in the first two chapters of Genesis as literally true. But there is a sliding scale of biblical inerrancy for they regard the eating of the apple by Eve as symbolic. Langson Gilky, distinguished theologian at the University of Chicago, has this to say: "The best kept secret of American Christendom is that the mainline churches never have had any trouble with evolution".

Fundamentalists can count on never having to change their minds. Those marching under the banner of "scientific" creationism should realize that the battle for the creation of the earth 6,000 years ago, the Noachian flood, and fiat creation of species has already been lost. But among fundamentalists it is virtue to believe in something in spite of evidence to the contrary. In contrast, it is not in the nature of scientists to swear to a belief in the absence of evidence. The fundamentalist churches, lacking a Pope as ultimate authority, have erected the Bible as a paper Pope and insist on its inerrancy and infallibility. But the Bible is so elliptically written that even the Devil quotes scripture to suite his purpose.

The fundamentalists of the religious right, the ultras, are a formidable group which includes some 30 to 80 million Americans. According to Jerry Falwell, they operate 40 television stations, 1400 radio stations and 140,000 fundamentalist churches in the U.S.A. Six of the television evangelists rake in more than one million dollars a week. This includes Jerry Falwell, Oral Roberts, Pat Robertson and Jimmy Swaggert.

To fundamentalists the following doctrines are essential: The inerrancy of the Bible; the

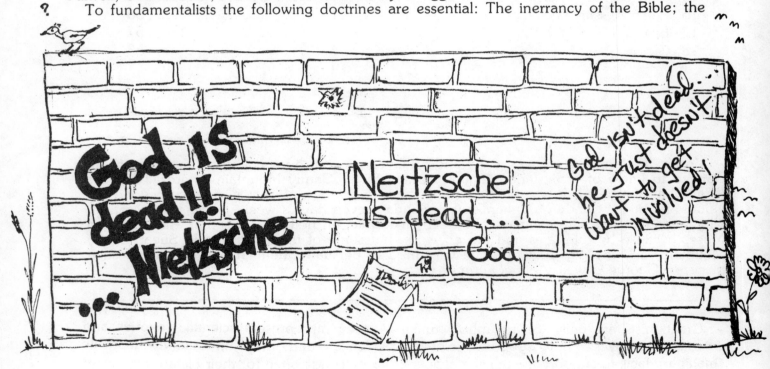

virgin birth of Christ; the atonement of Christ; the resurrection of Christ; and the miracle-working power of Christ. These are not dogmas which they really believe but only which they would like to believe. Fundamentalists political views are quite separate from their religious beliefs. Jerry Falwell's Moral Majority affirms basic principles: (1) opposition to abortion and euthanasia (2) pro-family — whatever that means; (3) pro-moral —according to their interpretation; (4) a strong hawkish national defense including support for Israel; (5) rabid anti-communism; and (6) anti-birth control or planned parenthoos. As in the Bible accounts, they believe that a woman should remain in her place and be weak, tempting and irrelevant.

"Send in your Love gifts."

Buy low sell high.

THE GURU IS IN

According to Barbara Hargroves of the Princeton Religious Research Center, the definition of a Christian used by fundamentalists is far more narrow than that used most commonly in our society. It tends to omit the majority of the members of the mainline protestant, or liberal churches, as well as most catholics — the majority of practicing christians. This majority of church members do not consider a literal interpretation of the biblical story of creation basic to their faith. Most are quite comfortable with an evolutionary understanding of the origin of the human species.

Creationists fit within that branch of Protestantism know as evangelism. Recent surveys have identified evangelicals as those who give an affirmative answer to these three issues: (1) having been born again or having had a born-again conversion; (2) having encouraged someone to accept Christ as their saviour, and (3) believing in a literal interpretation of the Bible. Over-represented among evangelicals are women, nonwhites, persons with less than a college education, southerners, older people, rural residents, and those below average on the economic scale. A vulnerable mix.

In keeping with the Fairness Doctrine, TV networks try to air both sides of any controversy question. There is one glaring exception to this usual presentation of balanced views--for example on prayer in schools. This is the role of televangelists who are free to hire airtime to praise, excoriate or "heal" the sick as they please while pandering for money. Their right to proclaim religious views without rebuttal is protected by law. Increasingly many use TV to discuss politics which should, in principle, cancel their tax exempt status. They, more than anyone else, enjoy unchallenged broadcast freedom of speech which is an important reason for their influence.

Modern science has not written the obituary to fundamentalism, although many scholars have predicted its imminent demise. The fundamentalists, to return the favor, have predicted the speedy end of the world. The reason for their remarkable resilience is, no doubt, that in the nuclear age this prediction now seems uncomfortably close to the mark — least to some persons.

2

MIRACLES

Some creationists believe that during creation week, many normally impossible things happened — but after the seventh day miracles ceased. They argue that natural laws came into effect only after Adam and Eve sinned. This exemption from natural law during creation week is hardly enough as the Bible recounts numerous miraculous happenings -- e.g. Jesus walking on water. And churches, even today, recite a litany of the supernatural. Thousands of miraculous healings are reported from Lourdes, France (the Catholic Church itself only accepts seventeen).

Creationists John Whitcomb and Henry Morris wrote in "The Genesis Flood" that a spate of major miracles were needed to account for the Biblical Deluge. These Acts of God included: the revelation of the design of the ark to Noah; the gathering together and husbandry of the animal multitudes; the gushing of flood waters from subterranean springs; the collapsing of the watery Firmament above the earth; and the sudden appearance of mountains, continents and ocean basins. When miracles are let in the front door, science escapes out the back door since there is no way the Noachian Flood can be supported scientifically.

Creationists believe that in the beginning there were no meat-eating animals in the blissful Garden of Eden. But they also insist that the basic "kinds" have not changed or evolved since then. We are asked to imagine a created plant-eating lion developing into a meateater practically overnight without changing enough to be considered a different "kind". The science of genetics simply cannot support such a bizarre version of evolution and it is laughable that creationists should demand it. They either believe in radical evolution beyond the wildest dreams of evolutionists or they need to invoke another miracle.

The scientific method prohibits resorting to the supernatural. Science requires that results be obtained naturalistically — with less than one miracle. This does not necessarily mean that there is no such thing as the supernatural but only that the supernatural lies outside the realm of science. By and large, science seeks only proximal answers. Ultimate answers still elude all of us — religionists and scientists alike. It is better to leave question marks than to pretend to know.

Religion is a quare thing. Be itself it's all right. But sprinkle a little pollyticks into it an' dinnymite is bran flour compared with it. Alone it prepares a man f'r a better life. Combined with pollyticks it hurries him to it.
—Mr. Dooley (Finley Peter Dunne)

The clairvoyant perceives something that his client does not — namely, that he is an idiot.

How many evils have flowed from religion!
—Lucretius, 57 B.C.

SIXTEEN CRUCIFIED SAVIORS

Hereunder is a short list of some of the alleged "saviours" who came into the world, and preached and prophesied their delusions and were executed long before Jesus:

Salvahan of Caribec	100 B.C.
Quirinus of Rome	506 B.C.
Wittoba of Telingonese	522 B.C.
Prometheus of Greece	547 B.C.
Quezalcotl of Mexico	587 B.C.
Sakia of Hindustan	600 B.C.
Alkestus of Aegeia	600B.C.
Iao of Nepaul	622 B.C.
Indra of Tibet	725 B.C.
Bali of Orissa	725 B.C.
Hesus of Stonehenge	834 B.C.
Tammus of Syria	1100 B.C.
Crishna of India	1200 B.C.
Atys of Chaldea	1200 B.C.
Thulis of Egypt	1700 B.C.
Osiris of Karnac	2200 B.C.

Then there was Beli of the Afghans, Horns of Egypt, Baal of Phoenicia and Tyre, Zoroaster of Persia, Bal of Babylon, Kameloxis of Thrace, Zoar of Bonzes, Adad of Ninevah, Deva-Tat of Siam, Elaides of Thebes, Beddin of Japan, Cadmus of the Hellenes, Hel and Fata of the Mandans and Gentaut of the Aztecs--and many others.

All the above alleged "Christs" were "human sacrifices" remember. They gave their "lives and precious blood," for the sure and certain redemption of their believers.

Without the aid of a husband the following mythological young women bore a Divine Son:

Miss Yesoda	Mother of Chrishna
Miss Celestine	Mother of Zulis
Miss Chemalma	Mother of Quezalcotl
Miss Semele	Mother of Bacchus
Miss Prude	Mother of Hercules
Miss Alcemone	Mother of Alcides
Miss Shingmon	Mother of Yu
Miss Mayence	Mother of Hesus
Miss Mary	Mother of Jesus

Confucius, Zoroaster, Chrishna, Pythagoras, Mithra, and Sakia had angelic and shepherd visitors and their mothers were called by the devotees "Queen of Heaven." ---T.T. Woods *Contemporary American Writer.*

Man tends to be religious in the sense that his conceptualizations commonly involve awe, superstition and belief in the animistic, supernatural, and spiritual. The mind of man probably needs a certain amount of fantasy which commonly takes the form of local mythologies and fairy tales---Preston Cloud

There is convincing proof that William Shakespeare rather than Gideon wrote the Bible. The evidence lies in a cryptogram in Psalm 46. If one counts in 46 words from the beginning, the word "shake" appears. If one counts in 46 words from the end, one finds the word "spear." *Voila!* Bill Shakespeare wrote the Bible! He either did so or it was written by another man of the same name. At the very least, if Shakespeare did not write the Bible, he missed the chance of a lifetime.

3

PSYCHIC SURRENDER

Reality is scary — an enormous mechanistic universe ruled by chance and impersonal rules with vistas of vast space and endless time. It is more comforting to believe in a small, youthful world and to pray to God for personal guidance — a world in which you are His only concern and where you will not be consigned to Hell if you follow the Holy Word of a televangelist or your local guru. Science is dangerous, with its nuclear bombs, genetic engineering and poison gas. It may well be that civilization is disintegrating and the world is heading toward a nuclear holocaust. So why not turn to religion and await the Day of Judgement when all true believers will be lifted to eternal bliss — with the added joy of

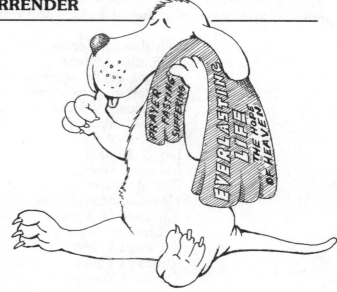

watching the scoffers writhe forever in torment. The end result is psychic surrender.

Psychic surrender can be defined as the act of turning complete control of your life and the responsibility of your total existence over to someone you believe is stronger and more capable than yourself. Psychic surrender is a form of symbolic suicide; you lose your life by giving it away. The rationale is that if life is a lie, and I am a part of society, then society is a lie. If I am crumbling, then society is crumbling. It is the methodology of fundamentalism.

A sizeable portion of the population has decided that their own search for meaning in life isn't worth it and have turned their lives over to gurus and shamans. Cultists are suspicious of the outside world and view it as foreign. If you can't change the world, change your perception of it. Life is a dream and an illusion. As with the Hindus, the purpose of

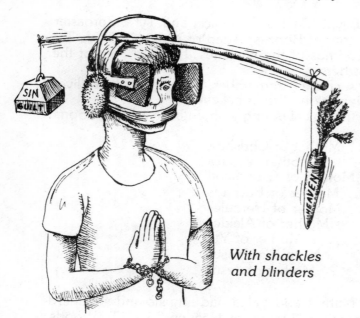

With shackles and blinders

life is to die and be re-incarnated into a higher caste. It would seem you have to be a fool to find happiness.

Cultists slavishly follow their masters who ride in their Rolls Royces, Mercedes and Lear jets. On the tv program "60 Minutes," Ed Bradley asked the Bhagwan Shri Rajneesh why he owned twenty-one Rolls Royces. The reply was: "Why not? It's a matter of no importance". By such irrational responses one can begin to understand the rise of off-the-wall cults such as the "Moonies" and the Scientologists.

Richard Lessner, on his final day as Religion Editor of the Arizona Republic, recently made some zany predictions about religion: (1) the U.S. Catholic bishops will stun the world by admitting they do not know anything about, will not publish a pastoral letter on, and have nothing to say in regard to the morality of Danish modern furniture. (2) Evangelist Billy Graham will hold his first ever Antarctic crusade. A meteorologist, three geologists and 2,200 penguins will be saved. (3) For the fourth consecutive year, the Episcopalian Church will produce no news of any kind.

FAIRLAWN NURSING HOME
SUNSET BEACH, CALIFORNIA

To: The Rt. Reverend Norman Vincent Glockenspiel

Dear Holiness;

Every Sunday on the Nursing home TV, I watch and listen Transfixed to your holy message from the Four Square Gospel Church. Your unquestioning faith inspires me. The Bible says it all. Glory! Why did God say he created Heaven and Earth in six days and Adam out of dust if he didn't? The world is full of Doubting Thomases, secular humanists, perverts, communists, evolutionists and other followers of Satan.

But God will prevail! Jimmy (send-in-your-love-gift) Swaggart believes in God. So does Oral (expect-a-miracle) Roberts. Likewise Jerry (the-sky-is-falling) What's-his-name. I'll never forget What's-His-Name. There, but for the grace of God, goes God.

You remember me, don't you, Eminence? In 1897, when I was eight years old, I wrote a letter to reporter Francis P. Church of the new York Sun begging to know if Santa Claus was Real. He replied, "Yes, Virginia, there is a Santa Claus... Because there is a God, there must be a Santa Claus ...") Would you believe it his letter has been reprinted in newspapers every year since then. Hallelujah!

I am 95 now, so soon I will ascend to Heaven. I know it is true because the church has promised it and they have all my money; Thank God for Medicare.

And by the way, Holy One, you may wonder if I still believe in Santa Claus. You can bet your sweet ass I do!

Yours in Jesus name,
Virginia

God placed our ears in just the right place on our heads, knowing full well that one day man would have to wear glasses. What better proof do we need of His provident design!...Rev. Billy Sol Cloudburst, 1956.

4

POWER OF PRAYER

In the Fortnightly Review of 1872, Sir Francis Galton (1822-1911) published a classic scientific study entitled *The Efficacy of Prayer*. In this work, he initially recognized that those religiously disposed petitioned in prayer for both spiritual and temporal blessings. By careful statistical studies he, a religious man, hoped to demonstrate the power of prayer. Declining to deal with isolated or anecdotal examples, which would be open to bias by the investigator, he examined large samples which could be guided by averages. He hoped to test his statistical prowess. He found, contrary to expectations, that sick persons who pray do not recover more rapidly than those who do not. There was no evidence that prayerful people had a better prognosis.

Galton then inquired into the longevity of prayerful versus non-prayerful persons. Extracting the data from biographical dictionaries of eminent members of certain professions,

*"I know that love
is the answer, but
what's the question?"*

he found no statistical difference between the longevity of clergymen, lawyers and doctors. In fact, there was a non-significant inverse trend whereby clergymen lived an average of 66.4 years, lawyers 66.5 years and doctors 67.0 years. Galton concluded that, "The prayers of the clergy for protection against the perils and danger of the night, for protection during the day, and for recovery from sickness, appear to be futile." Likewise, he found that public prayer for the sovereign of a state and the daily singing of "God Save the King" by British children was completely ineffectual as kings or sovereigns are the shortest lived of all those who have the advantage of affluence. Their average age at death is 66.0 years.

Galton noted that if prayerful habits influence temporal success, it was probable that insurance companies would offer a significant allowance for it, but no insurance companies ask questions of applicants about their private or family devotion. Nor do insurance companies take into account the relative risks run by ships and buildings owned by religious bodies. Zealots consider that it shows mistrust in God to put lightning rods on churches, but statistics on fires showed that they are good protection. Galton concluded that many items of ancient faith were simply superstition — the laying on of the hands by the sovereign, the burning of witches, ordeals by fire, and the miraculous power of church relics. He suggested that the civilized world should give up all belief in the efficacy of prayer as the evidence is consistently negative. The burden of proof rests with the believers.

Recently, America has launched a determined effort to upgrade our schools, especially in mathematics and the sciences, so as to be competitive with other technologically advanced countries such as Japan and those of Europe. Simultaneously there is also an effort to enact legislation sponsored at the presidential level to bring daily prayer into the schools. One congressman has suggested this is unnecessary because, "So long as there are math tests, there will be prayers in our schools." This is true, but do such prayers increase math scores? Perhaps the National Science Foundation should fund a study on the "prayer effect" but, of course, they will never do any such thing. Could it be because religionists fear a negative result? They increasingly attribute mysterious qualities to God, Heaven and the Holy Ghost which they hope will place them beyond the glaring searchlight of scientific scrutiny.

5

MORAL MC CARTHYISM AND THE WACKO-RIGHT

Moral McCarthyism is now transforming our nation's political process into a theological battle between sinners and saved. The fundamentalists argue that anyone who disagrees with their viewpoint is immoral and ungodly. The God Squads on the idiotic fringe now demand their sectarian beliefs, dogmas and doctrine govern us all. Those who disagree with the religions ultra-right are branded anti-God, anti-family, and anti-country. Debate, dissent, and diversity have become un-American activities. John Buchanan of the People of the American Way has called this chilling result: "Moral McCarthyism". The GOP has been denoted as God's Own Party and the Prayer Party, while their political party opponents are labelled anti-Christian. They communicate a religious message of hate and intolerance. Among the 12 members of Congress receiving a 100 percent Christian rating on the *Christian Voice* report cards are two representatives who were convicted of federal crimes, and one who was censored for having sex with a teenaged Congressional page. No religious group has the right to use the instruments of government to promote its creed.

Fundamentalists have coined the term "secular humanism", a radical right buzzword, now almost synonymous with Communist or fellow traveler. In our textbooks they would like to present history the way they would like it to be, but not the way it really was. The Moral Majority, Inc., is a form of neo-McCarthyism. They would like to be keepers of our ethics. In the early fifties, McCarthy searched for communists under every bed and now the neo-McCarthyites ferret out secular humanists — a label that remains undefined.

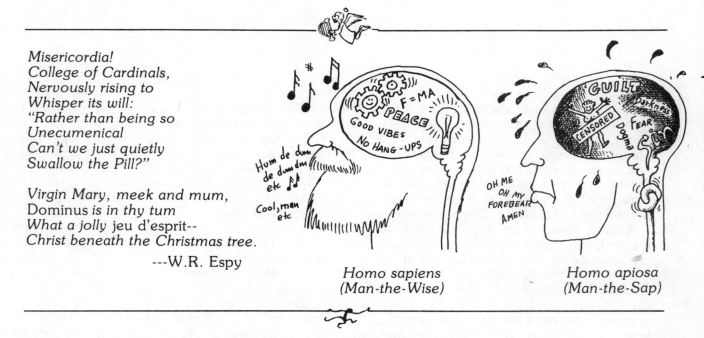

Misericordia!
College of Cardinals,
Nervously rising to
Whisper its will:
"Rather than being so
Unecumenical
Can't we just quietly
Swallow the Pill?"

Virgin Mary, meek and mum,
Dominus is in thy tum
What a jolly jeu d'esprit--
Christ beneath the Christmas tree.

         ---W.R. Espy

Homo sapiens
(Man-the-Wise)

Homo apiosa
(Man-the-Sap)

A BRIEF HISTORY OF MOHAMMEDISM:

About 600 AD a poor camel driver named Mohammed declared there was but one god, Allah; and Allah, to return the favor, declared there was but one prophet, namely Mohammed. Armed with this assurance, Mohammed (like Christ) set out to convert the world. Like Christ he had to flee to save his life, but unlike Christ he escaped to Medina and established his arrival there as year 1 on the Muslim calendar. And unlike Christ, he did not just hang around with men because it gave the wrong impression. Actually he married a rich widow and lived happily ever after.

In his spare time, Mohammed wrote the Koran, which, unlike the Bible, is not a synopsis of hundreds of different writings by anonymous authors. He actually wrote it himself. So we know where, when and by whom it was prepared. Most unusual.

6

AMRCS DLGNT CNSRS: BOOK BANNERS

History has been plagued with book burners, but certainly the most heinous event was the destruction of the great library of Greek classics at Alexandria in the mid-seventh century. The books were destroyed by the order of Omar the Caliph who said: "...if these writings of the Greeks agreed with the Book of God, they are useless, and need not be preserved: if they disagree, they are pernicious, and should be destroyed." In 642 A.D., the manuscripts of the library were distributed to the city's public baths whose four thousand furnaces were fueled for six months with these papyrus and parchment scrolls. The destruction of these texts was a tragedy of great moment, for it apparently contained the complete published works of Aeschyulus, Sophocles, Polybius, Livy, Tacitus, and hundreds of others which now reach us only in mangled form. There were full texts of the pre-Socratic philosophers and thousands of volumes in Greek, Egyptian and Roman history, science, literature and philosophy. In more recent times, the public torching of books was ordered by Adolph Hitler.

Today, book censorship is once again abroad on the land fostered by the fundamentalists. The shibboleth coined by the religious far right, "secular humanism," is used to tag any writings which are unacceptably man-centered rather than God-centered. Chief targets are books which mention evolution or the ancient age of the earth as these concepts conflict with creationism. With Ronald Reagan as their standard bearer and Evangelist-in-Chief, the religious "ultras" are pounding at the gates of our schools. Of the three R's they would replace 'Rithmetic with Religion. Book banning, burning, and censorship are rampant. Caving in to this pressure, textbook publishers are practicing self-censorship by deleting any references to evolution.

In 1982, the Texas State Textbook Committee refused to adopt the top-rated World Geography textbook because it contained the following sentence: "...biologists believe that human beings, as members of the animal kingdom, have adjusted to their environment through biological adaption." The objections offered by the creationists for the textbook were: "Most people do not consider themselves animals, and many people, including scientists, do not believe that the Earth is millions of years old. The textbook is biased in favor of evolution. Many people believe that mammals were created, not developed." One critic objected to passages in all biology textbooks which identified humans as animals. Recently, Laidlow Brothers (Doubleday) bowed to creationists demands and deleted any mention of evolution from its high school text. The publishers said the subject was omitted "to avoid the publicity that would attend any controversy". Textbooks which mention evolution in Texas must contain a disclaimer on the inside fly leaf to the effect that evolution is not a fact but only a theory.

In one textbook, the sentence: "No one knows exactly how people began raising plants for food, instead of searching out for wild plants..." was changed because of the following objections: "The text states theory as fact, leaving no room for other theories, such as the Biblical accout of Cain as a farmer." In another text book, the statement, "the great mountain ranges of the world were not formed at the same time" was modified because of the following objection: "The text presents theory as fact. Many people do not believe that

"Beware of false prophets, who come to you in sheep's clothing but inwardly are ravenous wolves." — Matthew 7:15.

the earth is as old as is implied here."

Censorship of science textbooks has been practiced by creationists for more than fifty years. Apparently, most publishers are collaborating with the censorship practice in Texas, which is the second largest textbook purchaser in the nation. The effect is nationwide, because publishers cannot afford to maintain two separate editions. A publishing executive is quoted as saying: "You are not going to find the word 'evolution' in our next textbook *Experiences in Biology.* Our reason for self-censorship is to avoid controversy. We would like to sell thousands of copies."

In 1981, the Alabama Board of Education banned the textbook: *Unfinished Journey: A World History* by Marvin Pervy. They objected to the following passage: "...During the longest intervals of the Stone Age, humans developed a spoken language and learned how to make use of tools." The objection in this case was as follows: "...how does the author know that there was no language in the beginning? That is a very subtle way of telling us we evolved through evolution. This cannot be proven as fact, but is being stated as fact. There must have been language in the beginning, because Adam named all of the animals." The absurdities are so great one wonders why they conduct such a desperate wagons-in-a-circle defense of the literal truth of Genesis. A dose of Menckenian scorn seems in order: "If people choose to believe that Genesis represents an account of creation of the natural world, they should be free to do so. They should not, however, be free to impose creationist views upon others."

Often wrong, but never in doubt.

"I would not just ban *my* books, I would ban all books" ... reply by author Dashiel Hammet to Senator Joseph McCarthy at his Communist witch hunt trials, 1953.

If there *is* one focal point — one *key* element in the Religious Right's strategy, it centers on public education. And most specifically — the children. Tim LaHaye, a leading spokesman for the movement to "christianize" teaching methods plainly stated the objective: "We are in a battle for their minds." Jerry Falwell goes even further: "Good Christians, like slaves and soldiers, ask no questions." By mounting an all-out effort the Far Right hopes to *intimidate* administrators, teachers and publishers across the nation into accommodating their attempt at "mind control" — at indoctrinating children with a radical right wing ideology they falsely call "Christian." The first line of attack centers on *textbooks.* The far right claims that the majority of textbooks used in America's classrooms violate "Biblical Christian morality" and thus their religious freedom — that they are anti-Christian, anti-family, and favor one world government... They don't want children taught *how* to think, but *what* to think. Anything else is "secular humanism." Anthony T. Podestra, People for the American Way

7

TRUTH IN PACKAGING: VARIOUS VERSIONS OF CREATION

There is a deceitful tendency to call things what they are not. A good example were the so-called Fair Trade laws of the 1950's which were subsequently declared by the courts to be in restraint of trade and therefore illegal. These laws forbade discounting and so were highly favorable to the retailer but ripped-off the consumer. Another effort to deceive the public is provided by the title of the Institute for Creation Research of San Diego, California. There is no truth in packaging here as this institute does no proper research; is engaged in pseudo-science and promotes only a single version of special creation; namely, biblical creationism or the creation of the universe, the earth and life according to Genesis. Perhaps the best

Christian versus Marquesan myth of creation.

definition of a scientist is one who publishes his research results in a standard refereed scientific journal of which there are about 3,000 in English alone. By this definition those who work in the various creationist institutes do not qualify.

Another San Diego organization is called the Creation Science Research Center (CSRC). This title is a good example of Orwellian doublespeak because it is not concerned with creation themes in general but again only with that special variety — biblical creationism. The LaRouse *Encyclopedia of Mythology* contains several hundred creation scenarios. For example, the Romans trace their origins to Romulus and Remus who were discovered and raised by a female wolf. The Haida and Tlingit Indians of the Alaska panhandle regard the raven as God and this bird created man. Should we not teach these versions of creation as well? Any course in creationism should cover all versions. CSRC does not engage in science but pseudo-science akin to astrology and phrenology. It also does no research in the scientific meaning of that term. A more truthful name would be the Biblical Creationism Anti-Science Propaganda Front.

The Marqueses Islanders of Polynesia have still a different version of creation: "In the beginning, there was nothing. There arose a swelling, a ferment, a black fire, a spinning of vortices, a bubbling, a swallowing — there arose a whole series of pairs of props, posts or piles, large and small, long and short, crooked and bent, decayed and rotten. Similarly there arose pairs of roots, large and small, long and short, and so forth: there arose countless and infinitely many supports. Above all, there now arose the ground, the foundation, the hard rock, there arose the space for light, there arose rocks of different sorts." (From K. von den Steinen (1898) *Reise nach den Marquesas Inseln:* — Verhandl, Ges. Erdkunde zu Berlin, v. 25, pp. 489-513).

Yet another version of special creation is: the first bacteria might have been brought to earth 3.5 billion years ago by little green men from the planet Krypton in a flying saucer. They returned 3 billion years ago and found, "It was very good". So they dropped off some blue-green algae 400 million years ago. Then four million years ago they brought *Homo sapiens* or humans. This version is fully logical as the biblical version plus it has the advantage of being consistent with the geological record. Of course, it would have taken a few million trips just to fly all the species now living on earth. This scenario would seem to dull Occam's razor — the Principle of Simplicity.

Unlike organizations involved in propaganda (e.g. Moral Majority, Pro America, etc.) the missions of scientific societies are readily understood by their titles — American Association for the Advancement of Science, Geological Society of America, etc. Arizona State University has a recognized student organization whose anti-creationism stance is clearly apparent as its name is *Americans for Promoting Evolution Science* with the acronym of APES. This is truth in packaging!

The trouble with born-again Christians is that they are an even bigger pain the second time around. ---Herb Caen

---

Allan Frank of the *Washington Star* approached Senator Barry Goldwater with one last question: "What do you, Mr. Conservative, think about Jerry Falwell's statement that all good Christians should be against Sandra Day O'Connor's nomination to the Supreme Court", he asked. "I think every good Christian ought to kick Jerry Falwell's ass", replied the senator from Arizona. Nobody before had voiced such blunt outrage in such earthy American idiom, and nobody could have said it so effectively as this man from the right's own ranks. A few days later he entered into the record of the U.S. Senate an eloquent speech, "To Be a Conservative" which read in part, "I'm frankly sick and tired of the political preachers across this country telling me as a citizen that if I want to be a moral person, I must believe in "A," "B," "C," and "D." Just who do they think they are? And from where do they presume to claim the right to dictate their moral beliefs to me? And I am even more angry as a legislator who must endure the threats of every religious group who thinks it has some God-granted right to control my vote on every roll call in the Senate. I am warning them today: I will fight them every step of the way if they try to dictate their moral convictions to all Americans in the name of conservatism."

THEORY VERSUS FACT

Religions offers unquestioned answers. Science offers unanswered questions.

Creationists commonly make their case seem plausible by abusing the word *theory* as it is used in science. In their usage a *theory* is only an unsubstantiated speculation or guess. In science a theory is a coherent body of tested and confirmed knowledge. Evolution is not "just a guess" but a theory in the strictest scientific sense.

Evolution is both a theory and a fact. The fact is that life has clearly changed over the aeons as revealed by the fossil record while the theory of evolution attempts to explain why this has happened. Hypotheses whose predictions are verified by observing the real world obtain the status of theories. A prevailing principle or theory which helps define the entire structure of a particular science is called a paradigm.

Gravity is a good example. The *fact* is that objects fall down — toward the center of the earth. The *theory* as to why this happens is not fully understood even today. It was initially explained according to Isaac Newton by the attraction between masses. But this has recently been supplanted by Einstein's relativistic version even though Newtonian theory served us well for three centuries. Theories are not fixed but they evolve or change with time.

In the life sciences, evolution is not just an ordinary theory, but the "theory of theories" or the Grand Theory. It is the great ordering enlightenment and the central organizing concept of biology — a paradigm. As Nobel Laureate Theodosius Dobzhansky has aptly written, "Without evolution there is no biology."

In scientific philosophy there are no absolute facts but there are hard facts and evolution is one of these — as certain as the earth being a sphere and not flat. Since Charles Darwin first originated the concept of evolution six score years have passed. It is said that the sum total of scientific information doubles every fifteen years. Accordingly the data on evolution has increased one-thousand-fold. This information has been tested and retested and the general concept or theory of evolution has been sustained. The statement by Jerry Falwell in his infamous interview with *Penthouse* magazine that "There is not one iota of evidence in favor of evolution" is patent nonsense. It is apparent that creationists are not convinced by evidence, but only by faith. The facts be damned! They are also not interested in reality but only in believing in what feels good. More than 100,000 scientific papers have been published over the last century but all this evidence is dismissed by fundamentalists with a wave of the hand.

As Stephen Jay Gould writes, "In the common vernacular, 'theory' often means an imperfect fact or a guess. The creationists trade on this duality and confusion of meaning of the word theory. This usage is widely accepted in non-scientific circles. President Ronald Reagan said in 1980 regarding evolution, 'Well, it is a theory, it is a scientific theory only, and it has been challenged in the world of science — that is, not believed in the scientific community to be as infallible as it once was'. One hopes that this was simply campaign rhetoric. Well, evolution is a theory. It is also a fact. And facts and theories are different things, not rungs in a hierarchy of increasing uncertainty. Facts are the world's data. Theories are structures of ideas that explain and interpret ideas. Facts don't go away when scientists debate rival theories to explain them. Einstein's theory of gravitation replaced Newton's in this century, but apples didn't suspend themselves in mid-air pending the outcome. And humans evolved from ape-like ancestors whether they did so by Darwin's proposed mechanism, or by some other theory yet to be discovered".

PLAYING IT SAFE: PASCAL'S WAGER

A familiar refrain of the clergy is similar to that recited by the 17th century French philosopher, Blaise Pascal. He asserted that one should believe in the afterlife because it just might be true. If it isn't, you have lost nothing, but if it is, you have gained everything. So why not "play it safe"? The problem with this is: believe what? Every religious denomination contends that one must believe their way in order to reach the promised land. Some say that to reach Heaven, one must merely accept Jesus as one's savior. Others insist that various sacraments are required; and still others that baptism is obligatory. The "play it safe" approach would force one to adopt the beliefs of all of the various denominations or religions in existence. If you only accept a certain set of beliefs, you are no longer "playing it safe". You are gambling. You are betting that you have selected the correct road to salvation out of numerous paths that are available. These beliefs are mutually exclusive. From the Muslim perspective, all Christians are doomed to perdition and guilty of the grossest blasphemy. Any believer who follows Pascal and somehow thinks he is "playing it safe" is only deluding himself. Another problem is that an all-knowing God may damn anyone who bets on his existence only for the sake of prudence. And a truly wise God even may offer salvation only to freethinkers who doubt His existence.

I know that I am in touch with God because every time I pray I find I am talking to myself. — Rev. Jobst Grabenhorst, Backwater, Oklakansas.

"Dyslexia? What is lexdysia?"

There are numerous cases in societies where the Armies of the Night have ridden triumphantly over the minorities and established a powerful orthodoxy which dictates official thought. Spain dominated Europe and the world in the 16th century, but there orthodoxy came first. All divergence of opinion was ruthlessly suppressed. The result was that Spain did not share in the scientific, technological, and commercial ferment that bubbled up in other nations of Western Europe. Spain became an intellectual backwater for centuries. --- Isaac Asimov

10

A FAIRYTALE FROM THE BROTHERS GRIMM

An eight-year-old boy was asked by his mother what he had learned at Sunday school.

"Well", he said, "Our teacher told us about God sending Moses behind enemy lines to rescue the Israelites from the Egyptians. When they came to the Red Sea, Moses called for the engineers to build a pontoon bridge. After they had all crossed, they looked back and saw the Egyptian tanks coming. Moses radioed headquarters on his walkie-talkie to send B-17 bombers to blow up the bridges and save the Israelites.".

"Bobby", exclaimed his mother, "Is that really the way your teacher told you that story?"

"Not exactly, Mom, but if I told it her way, you would never believe it."

11

HENNY PENNY

"Goodness gracious me!" said Henny Penny, "The sky is falling! I must go and tell the king." The first End-of-the-World panic was presumably started in the old nursery fairytale. One day Henny Penny was hit on the head by something — perhaps an acorn. This convinces her that the sky is falling and she decides that she must dash off to tell the king. Along the way, she picks up a number of followers: Cocky Locky, Ducky Lucky, Goosey Lucy and Turkey Lurky, and finally Foxy Loxy. We are left in the dark as to what the king was supposed to do about this impending catastrophe. Recognizing gullibility, Foxy Loxy tells the others that he has a short cut to the king's palace. He leads them into his den where he eats them all except Henny Penny who "ran as fast as her little legs could carry her." The moral of this little tale is quite clear. Have a low gullibility index. Don't believe evangelists, gurus, shamans, fakirs or prophets who peddle stories about impending catastrophies. The prophets of doom abound.

*"The sky is falling!
The sky is falling!"*

To walk on water, you have to know where the rocks are. — Geologist's Dictum

Much of the Bible consists of obscene stories, voluptuous debaucheries, cruel and torturous executions and unrelenting vindictiveness.

---Thomas Paine, *Age of Reason*, 1803

The religion of one age is the literary entertainment of the next. --- Ralph Waldo Emerson.

What excellent fools religion makes of men. — Ben Johnson, 1603

The great mass of people are incapable of making individual judgements. They must rely upon faith alone. — Adolf Hitler in *Mein Kampf*

BETHLEHEM U.F.O.

Bright though it shines on Christmas cards, the Star of Bethlehem is dim to astronomers. They believe that there was no such thing because celestial bodies move predictively and their past positions can be charted over the millennia. The star is said to have enticed the Wise Men, but it is ignored by scientists. The Scriptures relate that the star which they saw in the east moved before them until it stood over where the Christ child was born but astronomical objects just don't do that. Biblicists have responded that it may have been a comet. Comets do move very slowly, but just don't ever stop. The star was supposedly so dazzling that the Magi took to their camels, yet King Harod had to ask them where it was. If the Magi were led to Jerusalem by a star seen in the east, they surely must have come from the west of the city or from the Mediterranean Sea. Boats rather than camels would seem more called for. As Arthur Hoag, Director of the Lowell Observatory in Flagstaff, Arizona exclaimed: "Balderdash! Astronomers dismiss the entire idea. In those ancient days, all stars were thought to presage the birth of important people."

What the churches teach and the preachers preach is either false or fallacious. The Christians have scattered tens of thousands of so-called truths, injunctions, principles in sermons, leaflets, and hymns; every one false, corrupting, enervating, emasculating, unreal, and injurious. All of these are out of the Bible, the most ruinous book ever written. Nothing ever furnished the same pabulum to imposters, sophists, scoundrels, and tyrants. — Edwin P. Reese

The real culprit behind the parade of evangelists is the Bible. As long as we believe that the Bible is a God-made book of facts instead of a man-made book of beliefs, we shall remain emotional and mental retardees.

13

$END YOUR LOVE GIFT

Some people collect stamps, rare coins, first editions or butterflies. I'm a collector of classic fund-raising letters from TV preachers. I have a thick file of letters that promise to cure all manner of aches and pains, create vast wealth, repel the godless communists, ward off evil spirits and roll out the red carpet to the pearly gates. All you have to do is send in a ten-spot and the miracle will occur.

My favorite is an old standard — The Sky-Is-Falling letter. It can take many forms, but the theme is always the same. Some vaguely defined — but always terrible — catastrophe is threatening the preacher and his flock. And the way to repel it, brothers and sisters, is for you to send money quick.

I'm pleased to announce that I have just added to my collection one of the finest The Sky-Is-Falling letters I've ever seen. It's a creation of evangelist Rex Humbard, one of the legendary veterans of the Bible-thumping trade. Humbard, who started as a traveling tent preacher in Arkansas many years ago, has long since shifted to TV and letter-writing computers.

I can understand his success when I look at a letter that he recently sent out. "Sister Jones: (the computers always personalize the letters) This letter is so confidential and important. After you read it would you please send it back to me?

"Sister Jones, please read this letter slowly and don't share it with anyone else. This is between God, you, Sister Jones, and me, Rex Humbard. You have no way of knowing the weight that is riding on these very words you are reading.

"Sister Jones, if someone whom you really loved was dying, if they needed a certain kind of medicine to save their life, and if you could get a bottle of this medicine to them, I believe in you enough to believe that, someway or somehow, you would get the money for that bottle of medicine. I don't believe you would let anything stop you from getting the medicine to save the life of the one you loved.

"Well, Sister Jones, I feel that I am like the person who is dying. I have fought the devil for 50 years! And now the devil, through a certain situation, has declared war on me *like you wouldn't believe!*

"He and his demons would like to silence Rex Humbard forever and they are *about to do it.* I can't write in this letter what is about to happen and I will not mention this on your TV program. As I said, this is between God, you and me.

"If I don't hear from you immediately the doors of my ministry, which have been wide open for 50 years, are about to be slammed shut.

"Sister Jones, I have sounded the alarm, both day and night, against sin and wrong. But now the devil has gone all out with this attack to stop Rex Humbard. And I am dying inside as I tell you that it does look really, really bad.

"I can't tell you the whole story in this letter but I must tell you that if you don't answer this letter, Rex Humbard and our church services through the mail and on television, which God is using to save people from a devil's burning hell, and all the good we are doing, feeding orphans and all the other things we are doing for God, may disappear from the face of this earth.

"It is an absolute emergency that I hear from you...I must have an answer...and God knows I must hear from you right away. Your answer will be this bottle of medicine for this dying person, 'God's Ministry.' You are going to be doing so much for so little, and God can help you to do your part."

He then goes on to a long and fervent prayer that God will help Sister Jones find $25 so she can send it to him. And he says that he and his wife are going to stay on their knees praying until they get the letter, and presumably the $25. The letter ends with him and his wife on their knees praying that the devil will be defeated. But he never does explain the devil's strategy.

(Reprinted with permission) Mike Royko, Chicago Tribune.

THE THREE B'S

The charismatic evangelists lack schooling in the three "R's". Their forte is the three "B's" — britches, breath and Bible, as Lowell Streiker has noted in his book, "The Gospel Time Bomb".

Fundamentalism is a bastion of male dominance—or britches. Sect leadership is a path to tax-free wealth, power and television stardom. Wives are submissive home bodies, barefoot and pregnant. Education is not a requirement. All one needs is a copy of the most dangerous book ever written, the Bible. It confers instant power, prestige and influence.

The second B is breath. Evangelists love the sound of their own voice, and they only listen while they talk. One waits in vain for some kernel of wisdom in their touchy-feely psychobabble of air, wind, and smoke. (We already know that: Love is the answer. But what was the question?) Why face reality when fantasy offers comfort, security and assurance. You can hear them talking but you can't hear them saying anything. But it seems bad breath is better than no breath at all. Nothing is more exasperating than waiting for a televangelist to say something. And, like things of the Lord, these sermons endure forever.

The third B is the Bible, that ancient, archaic, and cryptic book of mythology that virtually nobody reads. Sect leaders read underlined excerpts which constitute no more than five percent of the text. They wouldn't dare read, for example, Numbers 31 which unfortunately is all too intelligable. But with this book in hand one can instantly become an expert for telling someone else how to live and learn the truth while contemplating your navel! Go into a trance and have visions, witness miracles, and spout Bible-speak! Cecil B. deMille would have understood this.

"What could I have went and said that everyone looked at me so queer-like?"

Deity Overload?

It may be that, somewhere in the United States, some candidate who has prayed mightily for his own election and has assured his followers of divine support, is about to find in his mailbox a neatly typed but unsigned card that says: "I don't do city council elections."--- Calvin Trillin

15

19th CENTURY CULTS

There are four 19th century cults which have evolved (excuse the word) into established churches — the Mormons, the Christian Scientists, the Seventh Day Adventists, and the Jehovah's Witnesses. Their success appears to have been in direct relation to the incredibility of their dogmas which are but a source of amusement to the rest of the world.

We are asked to believe that Joseph Smith received the Book of Mormon as a stack of golden plates buried in a hill near Palmyra, N.Y. which later disappeared as miraculously as they appeared. With all the credibility of a spokesman from the Tobacco Institute, the Christian Scientists tell us that with pure faith one can cure cancer or a compound leg fracture. Like the modern evangelists, they practice medicine without a license.

The God squads are out witnessing again.

As we approach the year 2000, we can expect the warnings of the impending Apocalypse to become evermore shrill. We can comfort ourselves with the knowledge that the end of the world has been predicted before; many, many times before. So far, the doomsday prophets have had a perfect score — they have never been right. --- Daniel Cohen

The problem of such religions is that their dogmas are set in concrete — medical science has evolved in the past century but not the mind over matter dogma of Christian Science. The warning is apt: "Caution! My karma may run over your dogma." All four of these cults reject evolution in favor of biblical special creation. Only the Mormon Church is officially neutral although their rank and file is unaware of it. In 1956, then President and Prophet Wm. Stanley issued a statement stating that the Mormon Church (the Church of Jesus Christ of Latter Day Saints) takes no position either for or against evolution.

Incidently, the Roman Catholic Church, a few decades ago, adopted a position favoring evolution, bringing this church out of the Dark Ages. Subsequently, the hierarchy has been mighty careful not to disturb the tender minds of their sheep with this radical concept. Apparently, unlike God, religious dogmas are not immutable.

The Seventh Day Adventists and Jehovah's Witnesses are so lumped together as to be indistinguishable to the outsider. They are concerned with such minutiae as to whether the Sabbath falls on Sunday, Saturday, or whenever. Friday is ruled out as the Muslims have taken over this day.

"Your karma just ran over my dogma!"

The Devil stirs up arguments and quarrels, arms the murderer against his brother, urges rebellion, foments war, brings to birth storms, hail and diseases.... If there were no one but him, we would not have grain in our barns, not an obole in our purses and in front of us not one hour of assured existence.

Snakes and monkeys are subjected to the demon more than other animals. Satan lives in them and possesses them. He uses them to deceive men and to injure them. Demons live in many lands, but particularly in Prussia . . . In Switzerland, not far from Lucerne, upon a very high mountain, there is a lake which is called Pilate's Poole. There the Devil gives himself up to all kinds of infamous practices. In my own country, upon a high mountain called Poltersberg, there is a pool, If one throws a stone into it, instantly a storm arises and the whole surrounding countryside is overwhelmed by it.

This lake is full of demons; Satan holds them captive there. A large number of deaf, crippled and blind people are afflicted solely through the malice of the demon. And one must in no wise doubt that plagues, fevers and every sort of evil and calamity come from him . . . As for the demented, I hold it certain that all beings deprived of reason are thus afflicted only by the Devil. ---Martin Luther, 1483-1546, *Founder of the Protestant branch of Christianity*

Religion must destroy reason before it can introduce faith and it must destroy happiness before it can introduce salvation. Religion has a vested interest in misery, and it captializes on human suffering. It says in effect, "Go forth, sacrifice, and be miserable, as your reward is in heaven." This is a safe promise because the dead cannot return and ask for a refund. Christianity has insured its own existence by perpetuating human suffering.

Religion is regarded by the common people as true, by the wise as false, and by the rulers as useful.---R.W. Sellars

16

VIEWS OF PERCY BYSSHE SHELLY (ENGLISH POET, ca. 1830)

According to the Bible, God created Satan, who, instigated by the impulses of his nature, contended with the Omnipotent for the throne of Heaven. After a contest for the empire, in which God was victorious, Satan was thrust into a pit of burning sulphur. On man's creation, God placed within his reach a tree whose fruit he forbade him to taste, on pain of death; permitting Satan, at the same time, to persuade this innocent and wondering creature to transgress the fatal prohibition.

The first man yielded to this temptation; and to satisfy Divine Justice the whole of his posterity must have been eternally burned in hell, if God had not sent his only Son on earth, to save those few whose salvation had been forseen and determined before the creation of the world.

God is here represented as creating man with certain passions and powers, surrounding him with certain circumstances, and then condemning him to everlasting torments because he acted as Omniscience had forseen, and was such as Omnipotence had made him...

The penalties inflicted by that monster Constantine, the first Christian Emperor, on the pleasures of unlicensed love, are so iniquitously severe, that no modern legislator could have affixed them to the most atrocious crimes. This cold-blooded and hypocritical ruffian cut his son's throat, strangled his wife, murdered his father-in-law and his brother-in-law, and maintained at his court a set of blood-thirsty and bigoted christian priests, one of whom was sufficient to excite the one-half of the world to massacre the other...

God expressly commanded Moses to invade an unoffending nation; and, on account of the difference of their worship, utterly to destroy every human being it contained, to murder every infant and unarmed man in cold blood, to massacre the captives, to rip up the matrons, and retain the maidens alone for concubinage and violation. At the very time that philosophers of the most enterprising benevolence were founding in Greece those institutions which have rendered it the wonder and luminary of the world, am I required to believe that the weak and wicked king of an obscure and barbarous nation, a murderer, a traitor and a tyrant, was the man after God's own heart? A wretch, at the thought of whose unparalleled enormities the sternest soul must sicken in dismay! An unnatural monster, who sawed his fellow beings in sunder, harrowed them to fragments under harrows of iron, chopped them to pieces with axes, and burned them in brick-kilns, because they bowed before a different, and less bloody idol than his own. It is surely no perverse conclusion of an infatuated understanding that the God of the Jews is not the author of this beautiful world. (See Exodus 32, 26; Numbers 31, 7-18; Deuteronomy 3, 6; Joshua 10; 2 Samuel 12, 29.).

On the Origin of Man

Creationists believe that man was instantaneously created by God, based on an account in a book called "the Bible."

Several thousand years ago, a small tribe of ingnorant near-savages wrote various collections of myths, wild tales, lies and gibberish. Over the centuries, these stories were embroidered, garbled, mutilated, and torn into small pieces that were then repeatedly shuffled. Finally, this material was badly translated into several languages successively.

The resultant text, creationists feel, is the best guide to this complex and technical subject.

---Tom Weller

On Miracles:

The so-called miracles of science are not miracles at all because they can be duplicated and, of course, they are by the millions — the TV, the telephone, the laser, the computer, etc. True miracles, as in the Bible, happen only once. A miracle would seem to be something which happens almost never — if ever.

Religions are like glow worms; they require darkness to shine in. — A. Schopenhauer, (1788-1860)

17

BIBLICAL MORALITY

Holding up the Bible as a paragon of virtue is like canonizing Charles Manson. From the Old Testament we get such moral teachings as: believers should kill non-believers who tempt them into worshipping other gods (Deut. 13: 6-9), murder of the innocent as punishment for the guilty (Exod. 12:29 and 20:5, Lev. 26:22, Num. 14:18, Deut. 5:9 and 23:2, Isaiah 14:21-22);slavery is fine (Exod. 21:7, Lev. 25:44), mass slaughter and genocide are acceptable practices sometimes ordained by God (Num. 31:7 and 31:17-18, Joshua 6:21 and 10:40), children who speak against their parents and people who work on the Sabbath should be put to death (Exod. 21:17 and 31:15, Lev. 20:9), tattoos are evil (Lev. 19:28), little kids who make fun of prophets should be torn apart by bears in the name of God (2 Kings 2:23-24) and God is directly responsible for all evil as well as good (Isaiah 45:7, Lam. 3:38, Amos 3:6).

From the New Testament we get: you should give away your property to anyone who merely asks for it (Matt. 5:40 and 5:42, Luke 6:30), it is acceptable to lie as long is it wins converts (Rom. 3:7, 1Cor. 9:20-23), women must keep their heads covered when praying and may not speak in Church or teach men (1Cor. 11:5 and 14:34, 1Tim. 2:12) and it is good for families to be broken up for the sake of Christianity (Matt. 10:34-36, Luke 14:26).

It is true that many ethical teachings most people agree with (i.e., murder and theft are wrong) are found in the Bible. But people don't agree with them simply for that reason. Ethics based on reason rather than revealed religion has been a field of study for several thousand years, and through it these basic principles have become a part of the cultural "common sense." --- Jim Lippard, Philosopher

In 1973, the creationists of Tennessee managed to pass an anti-evolution law (Chap. 377 of 1973 Public Acts of Tennessee). The law commanded that equal time be given for creationism if evolution is taught and that textbooks must contain a disclaimer to the effect that evolution is only a theory and not a fact. The teaching of all occult or satanical beliefs of human origin were also prohibited. Recognizing a problem here, the legislators, in their infinite wisdom, expressly excluded the Holy Bible as falling under this act.

Examples of Provident Design
1. God made rabbits with white tails to be easier to shoot by man.
2. The sun rises at the precise moment day begins.
3. Whether we are short or tall our feet precisely touch the ground. Proof of God's infinite wisdom.

Mary Baker Eddy, a.k.a. Mrs. Mary A. Morse Baker Glover Patterson Eddy, the founder of the 19th century cult of Christian Science was apparently hard on her husbands. After suffering a minor injury from slipping on ice in Boston, Mrs. Eddy claimed she was miraculously healed by Christian Science after the doctor told her she would be crippled for life. The doctor denied ever making such a claim. The doctrine espoused in her book *Science and Health* was largely stolen from her former mentor, a Mr. Quimby.

I have been through it all; Zoroasterism, Tao, branches of Catholocism and all the rest. God is found within man. I have concluded that there is a cosmic consciousness, but to get in touch with it, you have to reprogram the computer — your mind. --- Burl Ives, 1983

If Jesus was a Jew, why does he have a Mexican name?

18

GLOSSARY

Bigamist: (1) A person who twice gives up liberty in the pursuit of happiness. (2) A mistake in companion selection for which the Mormon Church judges the penalty of trigamy.

Christian Science: A church founded in the late 19th century by Mary Baker Eddy proficient in the curing of imaginary diseases.

Convent: A place of retirement for women who desire leisure to meditate upon the vice of idleness.

Faith: A belief without evidence in what is postulated by one who speaks without knowledge of things without parallel. --- A. Bierce

Fairy: An angel who has fallen into apostasy and hence given to dancing, games of touchlast, trivial pursuit and making fudge.

Fundamentalist: One who finds every word of the Holy Writ to be true, if not literally, then symbolically and mystically. When one finds a text convenient to his argument, it is quotable as ultimate proof. But when confronted with an apparent contradiction, he sails away upon the wings of a symbol, an analogy of hidden or recondite significance.

Joss-sticks: Small sticks of incense burned by orientals in their tomfoolary and in cheap imitation of certain rites of the orthodox Christian churches. --- A. Bierce

Mormonism: The afterclap of Puritanism. --- Ralph Waldo Emerson

Omen: A sign that something may happen if nothing does.

Passalorynchite: A member of an early Christian sect who took a vow of perpetual silence. Today the IRS accuse these people of forming "the underground economy". Unfortunately, they are now extinct in religious circles save for a few Trappist monks who can't sell their story to a publisher. Much to the consternation of decent society, fundamentalistic Christians are definitely apassalorynchitic.

Philosopher: One who learns less and less about more and more until he knows nothing about everything. The opposite is the *specialist* who learns more and more about less and less until he knows everything about nothing. Both are in contrast to the *theologian* who learns less and less about less and less until he is unable to make an honest living.

Prayer: A verbal supplication to God soliciting favors since He does not answer letters nor appear for photo opportunities. A classic example of God's response occurred in 1887 following a 7.2 earthquake in northern Mexico, just south of the Arizona Territory. This created a break in the earth 50 km long and 3 m high — the greatest quake ever affecting Arizona. The terrified peons of the Pueblo de Bavispe poured into the village church praying for salvation. God released another jolt causing the roof to collapse and dispatching 42 of the pious to the stygian nether world. The moral: Beware of praying in the company of sinners for "Lo, I am an angry God", Judges 7:13.

Revelation: The last (66th) of the canonical books of the Bible, the Apocalypse. The

Book of Revelation reverberates with retribution, reverie, revival, revocation, revolt, revivification, revulsion plus a sprinkling of woes and things that go bump in the night.

Revolutionaries: A group of persons organized to overthrow a government, upset the status quo or destroy the current culture; for example, the Daughters of the American Revolution.

Shaman: Sham man

Soteriology: (1) The study of salvation by belief in the legendary Jesus Christ. (2) The science of hygiene. In both definitions the solution is to take a bath.

Soul: A spirit which inhabits the more human of human beings of the genus *Homo sapiens* except for Hotentots. A soul is also accorded pet cats, but otherwise denied to the beasts.

Theory: (1) In creationist usage, something less than a fact — a guess. (2) In scientific usage, a generally accepted idea supported by a preponderant evidence that describes and predicts conditions in the natural world. A theory is a statement which elucidates an underlying pattern of nature, a pattern that makes sense out of a myriad of observations, is logically consistent, and holds true when tested. Theories never become facts, they explain a collection of facts. Example: the Theory of Evolution.

Trinity: The most sublime mystery of holy religion. In terming it incomprehensible, one displays an inadequate grasp of theological fundamentals.

Wine: A fermented concoction of the Devil, drunk by Christians during communion. The beverage of choice in the top three levels of Dante's Hell.

Truly man is the king of beasts, for his brutality exceeds theirs.---Leonardo da Vinci

A Catholic university is a contradiction of terms. --- George Bernard Shaw

Whenever I question the existence of God, the reply I receive is that this world is so wonderful it must have been designed by a Supreme Being. But when I question the existence of an afterlife, this world is said to be so bad that there must be another one ready to put things right! --- Barbar Smoker (President, English Secular Society)

Some things are so forbidden, they cannot be mentioned on the list of forbidden things.

Fundamentalists base their beliefs on authority and revelation which supersedes evidence. Scientists on the other hand, accept evidence as superior to both revelation and authority. --- Preston Cloud

Which books to include in the Bible was decided by a vote of the church. The Apocrypha were left out.

Those who opt for creationism are open-minded. But it is a matter of "Come on in, nobody is at home."

PART 3

CREATIONISM AND THE PHYSICAL SCIENCES

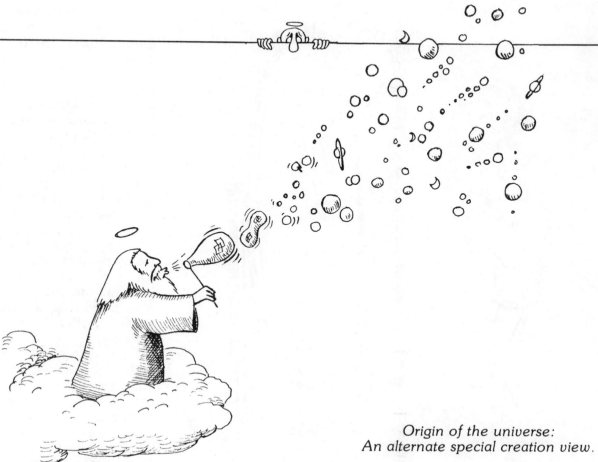

Origin of the universe:
An alternate special creation view.

1

BIBLE *VERSUS* PHYSICAL SCIENCE

The Bible according to religious prophecy has great scientific wisdom which man is now only beginning to realize. Critics, on the other hand, consider the Holy Writ to be its own worst enemy as it contains a plethora of statements therein which destroy any claims to scientific precision and which belong in the realm of mythology and folklore. Some are simply false while others are so vague it is impossible to know what is meant. Naturally apologists choose the more scientifically oriented interpretation.

The Bible speaks of the sun stopping for Joshua. Martin Luther and John Calvin took this as biblical evidence against the heliocentric solar system of Copernicus. Surely, they said, the sun must revolve around the earth in accordance with the Ptolemaic view. Creationists of bygone centuries, and some even today, offered two explanations for fossils in the rocks. One is that they were placed there by the Devil to deceive us and the second by God to test our faith.

To think clearly and freely is the best defense against religious tyranny. If we wish our schools to remain free and open to complex ideas against religious platitudes, we will have to fight to see that they remain so. After putting a man on the moon there is still a substantial contingent of bizarre creationists who believe that the earth was created in six days, 6,000 years ago, is flat, is fixed and does not rotate, and is the center of the universe.

The Dark Ages were terminated by the Renaissance and a scientific revolution sparked by the concepts of Nicolaus Copernicus, Johann Kepler, Galileo Galilei, and Isaac Newton. The very fabric of science was rewoven. The Polish astronomer Copernicus discovered the earth is not the center of the universe but instead travels around the sun. The revolution ended in

1697 when Isaac Newton described the motions of falling bodies and the gravitational paths of planets. Cherished concepts such as a flat and immovable earth had to be wrenched from their enshrinement in religious dogma.

A classical argument raged among the prophets of old concerning whether the sun was closest to the Earth at noon or at sunset. One faction claimed this distinction for high noon because proximity to the solar fire accounted for noontime being hotter. On the contrary, countered another group; the solar disk looms larger at sunset so the sun must be closer then. Early Christians remained in a quandary, being confused by the paradox that as one climbs a high mountain the temperature cools although one becomes closer to the sun. But about one thing they agreed, "The sun turneth to blood red as it settles into the earth because it looketh upon the blazing fires of Hell".

The biblical earth clearly is fixed, immovable and non-rotating and the Holy Writ was used by the Church to convict Galileo of heresy under threat of torture and execution. Joshua (10:12) commanded: "Sun stand thou still on Gideon, and thou, Moon, in the valley of Ajalon." Note that Joshua commanded the sun to stand still rather than the Earth to stop turning as is modern reality in our heliocentric solar system. In a similar vein in Ecclesiastes (1:5) we read: "The sun also riseth, and the sun goeth down, and hasteth to the place where he rose." And the Psalms (104:5 KJV) speak of the Lord who, "laid the foundations of the earth, that it should not be moved forever." In 1533, Martin Luther, objecting to Copernicus' astronomy, cited Joshua to prove that the earth was fixed.

In a public lecture a geophysicist explained how the earth floats in space supported by nothing at all. "This is possible," he explained, "because, although the earth has mass, the vector sum of its weight is zero." A creationist jumped to his feet waving his Bible and shouted, "This cannot be because the Bible, the Holy Word of God, tells us that the earth is immovable and rests on pillars; it has to be so!"

Hoping to gently defuse this zealot, the geophysicist asked, "What are these pillars resting on?"

After a moment of reflection the creationist retorted, "Other pillars, of course."

"And what, in turn are these pillars resting upon?" the geophysicist continued. Although at first perplexed, the creationist soon broke into a smile. "Its pillars all the way down!" he cried triumphantly.

The Catholic Church is not backward--a bit retarded perhaps, but not backward. We now know it is okay to eat fish on Friday. Galileo is about to be exonerated (but don't hold your breath) after nearly 400 years, for claiming that the earth is not fixed but spins on its axis and revolves around the sun. If you are confused about ethical sexuality just remember the basic rule is to do whatever produces more Catholics. The approved method for birth control is the rhythm method, a.k.a. papal roulette. But remember that the church until the 1920's had the timing exactly backward stating that the mid-period between the menses was the safe period.

I find it remarkable that Eve was in no way surprised to hear a snake talk.

I believe that we should remember the weekday and keep it wholly.

"You [Jerry Falwell] appear to be very religious, before your television audience. But inside, you are rapacious, unconverted wolves, seeking a greater share of the evangelical TV market, without really caring for the sheep you devour. You take money from widows and children, promising the blessings of God; it is the blessings of God you take from them, only to build an empire. You have a college where you pretend to free young men and women from the bondage of ignorance. What you really do is indenture them to platitudes and prejudices darker than their ignorance ever was. You make them twice the sons and daughters of hell they were when they came to you. You speak glowingly of the great numbers of people in your Sunday school, your services, and your extended programs. It is better to be right with ten persons than it is to be wrong with tens of thousands. You talk of legislating morality as if the Father had given you the franchise on morality and you knew precisely what it is. You hypocrite! Have you not heard that it is immoral to decide for others what they shall read and not read?"---Rev. John Killinger, First Presbyterian Church, Lynchburg, VA.

2

BIBLICAL EARTH *VERSUS* REALITY

Flat-earthism is a basic concept of Bible science. Old Testament verses clearly show the ancient Hebrews were flat-earthers. The Genesis creation story tells that the earth is covered by a vault and that celestial bodies move inside this firmament. This makes sense only under the assumption that the earth is flat.

In the Bible, we read, God "sits throned on the vaulted roof of earth, whose inhabitants are like grasshoppers" (Isaiah 40:21-22). He also "walks to and fro on the vault of heaven" (Job 22-14), which vault is "hard as a mirror of cast metal" (Job 37:18). The roof of the sky has "windows" (Genesis 7:12) that God can open to let the waters above fall to the surface as rain. The topography of the earth isn't specified, but Daniel "saw a tree of great height at the centre of the earth — reaching with its top to the sky and visible to the earth's farthest bounds" (Daniel 4:10-11). Such visibility would not be possible on a spherical earth, but would be expected if the earth were flat.

The earth is also flat in the New Testament. Matthew wrote, "The devil took Jesus to a

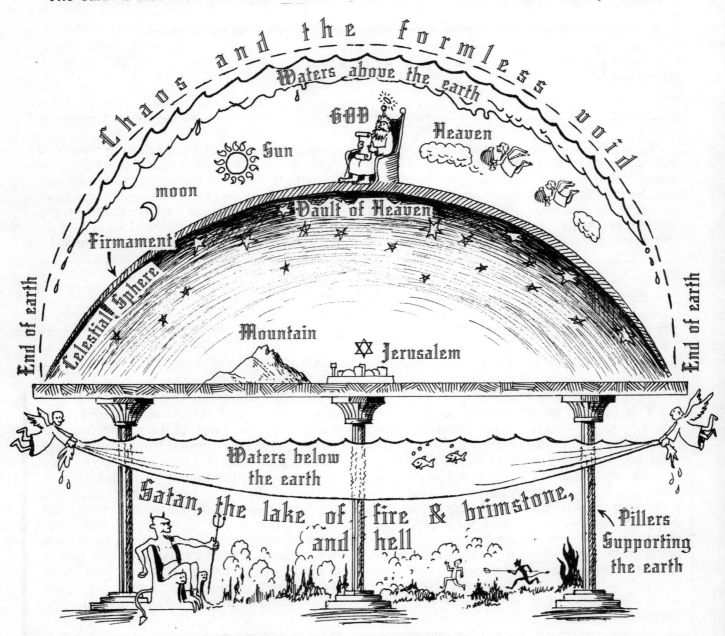

The Earth as depicted in the bible.

very high mountain and showed him all the kingdoms of the world in their glory." Even from a mountain of infinite height it would only be possible to see one half of a spherical earth. Finally, Revelations refers to "the four corners of the earth." Spheres lack corners. A tetrahedron, of course, does have four corners or coigns, but it is doubtful that biblical writers had this shape in mind.

While the Bible does not flatly state the shape of the earth, it repeatedly says in plain Hebrew that the earth is immovable (see, for instance, I Chronicles 16:30, Psalm 93:1, Psalm 96:10, and Psalm 104:5).

While priests found it relatively easy to ignore the flat-earth implications in the Bible and to adopt the spherical system of Ptolemy, they were rudely shaken by Copernicus and Galileo. Galileo, of course, was arraigned before the Catholic Inquisition and forced to recant his heretical view that the earth rotated and also revolved around the sun. For scriptural reasons other early Protestant reformers also rejected the Copernican system. These included Luther, Calvin and Wesley. Some Protestant creationists are still fighting a rear-guard action against heliocentricity.

Biblically, the earth is arched over with a solid firmament (Genesis 1:7). Isaiah and the Psalms state the heavens are stretched out "like a curtain" and again "like a tent to dwell in". The universe, then, resembles a simple house with the earth as the ground floor and the firmament as the ceiling beneath which God suspends the sun to rule the day and the moon and stars to rule the night. Waters or seas lie both above the firmament and beneath and surrounding the square or rectangular earth. Waters are let down upon the earth by the Lord and his angels through the "windows of heaven." Water also ascends to the earth through the "fountains of the deep". St. Augustine said it mattered little whether the celestial dome rested on pillars or hung over the edges on the earth.

The theologian Cosmas Indicopleustes identified the earth's basic geography based on scripture. The earth, he wrote, is rectangular, flat, and surrounded by four seas. It is four hundred days journey long and two hundred broad. At the outer edge of the four seas are massive retaining walls enclosing the entire earth and supporting the firmly attached vault of the heavens. Cosmas quotes the sublime words of Isaiah: "It is He that sitteth upon the circle of the earth,...that stretcheth out the heavens like a tent to dwell in"; and the passage in Job which speaks of the "pillars of heaven". Regarding the oceans, Cosmas uses the text in Genesis, "Let there be a firmament in the midst of the waters and let it divide the waters from the waters." And from Psalms he adds, "Praise him, ye heaven of heaven, and ye waters that be above the heavens." Angels, he avers, open and close the "windows of heaven" (Genesis) to provide rain. In summation, Cosmas declares, "We say therefore with Isaiah that the heaven embracing the earth is a vault, with Job that it is joined to the earth, and with Moses that its length is greater than its breadth.

If only God would give me some clear sign! Like making a large deposit in my name at a Swiss bank. — Woody Allen.

The popes, like Jesus, are conceived by their mothers through the overshadowing of the Holy Ghost. All popes are a certain species of man-gods, for the purpose of being the better able to conduct the functions of mediator between God and mankind. All powers in Heaven as well as on earth, are given to them. ---Stephanus V, *Roman Pope, 885-891*

The most remarkable achievement of the Jew was to impose on Europe, for eighteen centuries, his own superstitions. --- Thomas Huxley, 1825-1895

Send $$$! so I can buy Jesus more TV time so I can tell more people to send $$$! so I can buy Jesus more TV time so I can tell more people to send $$$$!....---Rev. Billy Sundaygraham

All people of antiquity regarded their own central city or holy shrine as the center of the flat earth. To the Muslims, it was Mecca and the sacred Kaaba stone; the Chinese regarded their empire as the Middle Kingdom; the Jews were no exception — the center was Jerusalem. Early Christians located it more exactly as the Holy Sepulchre within Jerusalem and stated that a spear thrust erect into the ground there cast no shadow at the equinox.

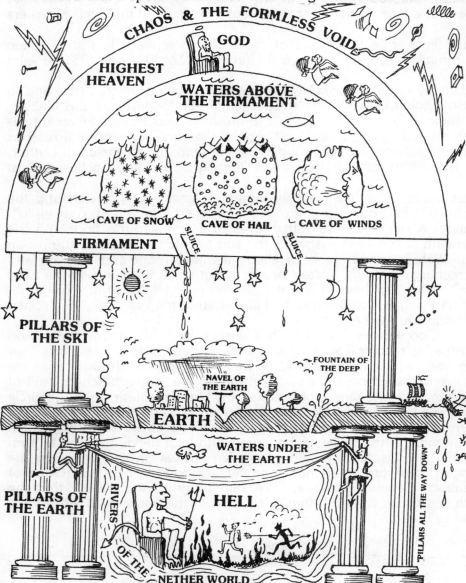

The ancient biblical view of the universe

In Genesis 1:6-10 (New American Bible) we read: "Then God said, 'Let there be a dome in the middle of the waters to separate one body of water from another.' And so it happened: God made the dome, and it separated the water above the dome from the water below it. God called the dome 'the sky.' Evening came, and morning followed — the second day. Then God said, 'Let the water under the sky be gathered into a single basin, so that the dry land may appear.' And so it happened: the water under the sky was gathered into its basin, and the dry land appeared. God called the dry land 'the earth,' and the basin of water he called 'the sea'."

Envisioned in this pre-scientific account is a flat terrestrial plain over which is erected the great crystalline firmament or dome of the sky. Water not only partially covered the earth but also formed a vast reservoir above the dome. And why not? This model accounted nicely for rainfall and explained why the sky is blue — the color of pure water.

In the ancient biblical view the universe was three storied. It consisted of the cavernous underground of Hades or Hell, the flat earth proper, and the sky-dome beneath which were attached the sun, moon and stars. It was quite natural to believe that stars fell from time to time and that there was a real and present danger of the sky itself falling. These themes occur throughout the Bible. See, for example: Genesis 28:12; Exodus 20:4; I Kings 8:35; Job 11:7-8; Psalms 78:23-24, 138:8, 148:4; Isaiah 7:10, 14:13-15; Ezekiel 26:19-20; Amos 9:2; Matthew 11:23; Romans 10:6-7; and Philippians 2:10.

On the peak of the firmament was, of course, the lofty house of God, from whence He viewed the comings and goings of man — and occasionally He descended in a whirlwind to

I don't want to achieve immortality through my work, I want to achieve immortality through not dying. --- Woody Allen make a personal appearance. The Tower of Babel (Genesis 11) depicts the fall of those mere mortals who tried to erect a tower for access to the third tier so as to invade Heaven and usurp the throne of God. The creationist, wedded to biblical inerrancy, has no choice but to accept this naive view of the world. By what logic can he accept the Noachian Flood but reject the three-tiered universe and the flat earth?

Although the concept of a flat earth is well-supported scripturally, most creationists do not want to be associated with this view. This is somewhat ironic since all flat-earthers are creationists. In fact, scientific creationism, geocentrism and flat-earthism are respectively the liberal, moderate, and conservative branches of the tree of "Bible science". The Bible is, from Genesis to Revelations, a flat-earth book. Creationists all agree on the usefulness of the Bible as a scientific text, the weakness of mere scientific theories, the duplicity of conventional scientists, and the impossibility of reconciling evolution with the Holy Writ. Creationists rarely express their suspicions in plain English, but they strongly imply that much of modern science is a fraud. Duane Gish of the Institute for Creation Research once told an audience: "I have yet to find a scientific fact which contradicts the Bible, the Word of God."

According to creationist Charles Johnson, President of the American Flat Earth Society, the U.S. Government will one day officially proclaim the earth to be flat. That great day, he believes, will also mark the downfall of evolution. Creationists know "in their hearts" that the earth is flat. In the mid 1960's NASA released the first deep-space photographs of the cloud-swirled, blue planet we call Earth. A reporter showed one of them to the late Samuel Shenton, the president of the International Flat Earth Research Society. Shenton examined it carefully and said, "It is easy to see how a picture could fool the untrained eye." Well-trained eyes programmed by indoctrinated minds characterize fundamentalists. Fantasy overrides reality.

The Holy Writ is crystal clear about the biblical model of the earth and no amount of apologetics, exegesis or hermaneutics can gainsay the concepts involved. Any claim to the contrary is deceitful.

Literalists take heed:
The reconstruction of a Tri-ass-ic dinosaur

The Christian God is a being of terrific character--cruel, vindictive, capricious and unjust...I read the Apocalypse and considered it merely the rantings and ravings of a maniac...What has not meaning admits no explanation.---Thomas Jefferson (1743-1826)

If books be confirmatory of the Koran, they are superfluous; if contradictory they are pernicious. Let them be burnt.---Khalif of the Saracens.

3

EARTH CREATION IN SIX DAYS: WOODCUT

On Day One, God created a formless earth, waters, light and darkness — the four basic elements.

On Day Two, He created the firmament, a crystalline dome over the earth to separate the waters above the earth from those below. (The waters above the firmament account for the blue color of the sky and when the windows of the firmament are opened rain falls).

On Day Three, the waters on the earth are gathered into seas and dry land emerges. God creates the first plants — grass, herbs, and fruit trees.

On the Fourth Day He creates the sun, the moon, and the stars — a bit unnecessary as God already created light and darkness on Day One. He let in the light each day and let in the darkness each night.

God's creation of the world in six days as described in the Book of Genesis (Chapter 1:1-31). Woodcut from a sixteenth century French Bible.

On the Fifth Day, God created animals including fish, fowl, and whales.

On the Sixth Day, He created cattle, beasts, and creeping things like snakes and other reptiles. And, most importantly, He created man in His own image. Actually the original Hebrew text reads *Elohim,* meaning gods; (this is the plural form of Eloha, meaning god). This passage was written while the Jews were still polytheistic.

This imaginative tale was believed by many people during the Dark Ages and remains today a delightful whimsy enjoyed by children.

From the beginning to the end, the Bible is a flat earth book, with the earth resting on pillars. It is left to our imagination as to how, in turn, the pillars are supported. The nether region houses Hell and the abode of Satan. There also is the lake of fire and brimstone into which are thrown all non-believers. There are also vast "waters beneath the earth" which fed the "fountains of the deep" inundating the land during the Noachian Flood. The earth is truly *terra firma* as it is fixed and immovable. Jerusalem is positioned at the center and nearby is a high mountain. Satan took Jesus to the top of this mountain from whence they could see all the kingdoms of earth (Matt 6:13). This, of course, would only be possible on a flat earth. The earth is described as having both corners and ends so its shape is probably square.

Covering the earth is a vast crystaline dome — the celestial sphere or firmament. Affixed to this dome are the stars which, in moments of anger, God causes to fall to earth. God himself sits on a white throne on the vault of heaven from where He can interfere with the goings on of man on a day to day basis.

Somewhere above the celestial sphere lies Heaven, the abode of saved souls which enjoy everlasting life. Above(?), too, are the sun and the moon which transit the stationary earth. Capriciously, by God's will, the moon sometimes turns to blood and the sun darkens, stops or reverses its motion across the sky. Nowhere in the Bible is there any mention of the planets.

There are also waters above the earth which provide rain and fed the Great Flood. Beyond is Chaos and the Formless Void having little useful purpose except as the abode of the extinct race of Pre-Adamites about which little is known. Presumably they provided a wife for Cain as Adam and Eve bore only sons.

Only in revealed religion does a mistranslation improve the sense.---W. Somerset Maugham.

Doubt is the beginning of wisdom. ---Clarance Darrow, Scopes Trial, 1925

God himself seemed to enjoy punishing myriads of people, usually through famine or disease, for rather minor offenses. For example, He killed 70,000 men because David took a census of Israel (II Samuel 24). He also lovingly (?) dispatched two bears to claw apart 42 children for mocking the prophet Elisha (II Kings 2:23-24). Such accounts abound in the Old Testament. Thomas Paine wrote: "Whenever we read the obscene stories, the voluptuous debaucheries, the cruel and tortuous executions, the unrelenting vindictiveness in the Bible, it would be more consistent that we called it the word of a demon rather than the word of God. It is a history of wickedness that has served to corrupt and brutalize mankind."

I would believe the Bible was the word of God if it contained so much as one single natural law expressed mathematically. A single formula sometimes elucidates more about the universe than an encyclopedia, e.g., $E = mc^2$, $F = \frac{1}{2}mv^2$, etc. The Bible does mention the relationship between the diameter of a circle and its circumference but gets it wrong. The value for the font (the Molten Sea) at King Solomon's Temple is given as 30 cubits around and 10 cubits across. The value of pi would then be 3.0 and not the correct value of 3.1416. One might argue that this is quibbling but remember the Bible is claimed not to speak in an approximate manner but to be absolutely and literally true.

4

SCIENCE CONFRONTS BIBLE EARTH

The ancient Hebrews, like their older and more powerful neighbors, the Babylonians and the Egyptians, were flat-earthers. The Hebrew cosmology is never actually spelled out in the Bible but, even without the Babylonian system upon which it is patterned, it can be read between the lines of the Old Testament. The Genesis creation story itself suggests the relative size and importance of the earth and the celestial bodies by specifying their order of creation. The earth was created on the first day and it was "without form and void" (Genesis 1:2). On the second day a vault — the "firmament" of the King James Bible — was created to divide the waters, some being above and some below the vault. Not until the fourth day were the sun, moon, and stars created, and they were placed "in", not "above" the vault. The sizes of these bodies are not specified, but they had to be small, as Joshua later commanded the sun to stand still "in Gideon" and the moon "in the Vale of Aijalon" (Joshua 10:12).

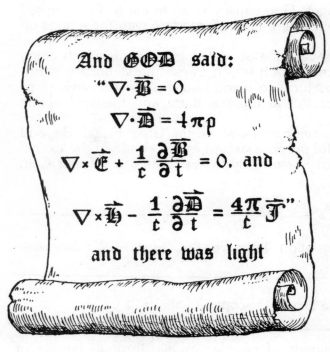

And G⊕D said:

$$\nabla \cdot \vec{B} = 0$$

$$\nabla \cdot \vec{D} = 4\pi\rho$$

$$\nabla \times \vec{E} + \frac{1}{c}\frac{\partial \vec{B}}{\partial t} = 0, \text{ and}$$

$$\nabla \times \vec{H} - \frac{1}{c}\frac{\partial \vec{D}}{\partial t} = \frac{4\pi}{c}\vec{J}$$

and there was light

Genesis 1:4 and
Maxwell's equations.

These passages, plus the more explicit astronomical section in the influential but noncanonical Book of Enoch led the more literal-minded early Christians to reject the idea of a spherical earth as heresy. Many of the fathers of the Church were flat-earthers, including Lactantius, Tertullian, and Clement of Alexandria. Gradually they developed a "scientific" flat earth system with which to oppose the Ptolemaic astronomy then becoming popular.

Claudius Ptolemy's *Almagest*, written about 140 A.D.,, was the culmination of six centuries of Greek astronomy. It wasn't until about 550 A.D. that Cosmas Indicopleustes published the alternate (flat-earth)system in his book *Christian Topography*. Cosmas, an Egytian monk, offered many of the same arguments used by the flat-earthers today, but he came to a different conclusion about the shape of the earth. Using a barrage of quotations from Scripture and from the fathers of the Church, Cosmas tried to show that the earth is a rectangular plane with its east-west dimension twice the north-south dimension. Sunrise and sunset, he suggested, were caused by a huge mountain in the far north. Cosmas fought a losing battle, and the ancient idea of a flat earth quickly lost ground. The Ptolemaic system of astronomy, based on a spherical earth, worked reasonably well. By the twelfth century, flat-earthism was essentially a dead letter in the west. (From *Science Confronts Creationism*.)

Regarding a flat earth:
The *Catholic Encyclopedia* quotes St. Augustine as writing: "As to the fable that there are Antipodes, that is to say, on the opposite side of the earth...men walk with their feet opposed to ours, there is no reason for believing it.

We have just enough religion to make us hate, but not enough to make us love one another. --- Jonathon Swift, 1706

5

BIBLICAL QUOTATIONS CONCERNING THE EARTH

1. (Math. 4:8) "Again, the devil taketh him [Jesus] up into an exceeding high mountain, and showeth him *all* the kingdoms of the world,…"
2. (1Chron. 16:30) "Fear before him, all the earth: the world also shall be stable, that it be not moved."
3. (Psalms 104:5) "[The Lord] *who* laid the foundations of the earth that it should not be removed for ever".
4. (Rev 21:1) The new earth is without any sea.
5. (Isaiah 34:4) "…, and the heavens shall be rolled together as a scroll:…"
6. (Isaiah 40:21) The earth has foundations.
7. (Isaiah 40:22) "It is he [the Lord] that sitteth upon the *circle* of the earth…that stretcheth out the heavens as a *curtain,* and spreadeth them out as a *tent* to dwell in."
8. (Isaiah 40:28) (and in many other biblical verses) "…the Lord, the Creator of the *ends* of the earth,…"

9. (Isaiah 38:8) The westward direction of the sun is reversed.
10. (Isaiah 45:6) The sun rises from the west rather than from the east.
11. (Isaiah 60:19) "The sun and the moon will no longer be a source of light".
12. (Isaiah 66:1) "The heaven is my throne, and the earth is my footstool…"
13. (Daniel 4:10-24) "A tree grows tall enough to reach the heaven, from whence *all* the earth can be seen".
14. (Joel 2:31) "Sun turned into darkness and the moon into blood".
15. (Amos 8:9) "Sun sets at noon". (An impossibility by definition.)
16. (Amos 9:5) Hand of God causes earth to melt.
17. (Habakkuh 3:11) "Sun and moon stood still in their habitation".
18. (Matt 24:29) "The stars shall fall from heaven".
19. (Rev 6:13) Stars fall to earth.
20. (Rev 7:1) Angels stand at the four corners of the earth.

6

AGE OF THE EARTH: USSHER *VERSUS* RADIOMETRIC DATING

An essential claim of creationism is "a relatively recent creation of earth and universe." By making calculations based upon the number of generations listed in the Bible, (the "begat method"), as many as 200 different scholars have individually decided that the earth had been created between 6,000 and 3063 B.C. — roughly 5,000 to 8,000 years ago. Early Christian scholars like St. Augustine believed the earth to be 6,000 years old by summing biblical geneologies. Shakespeare mentions this date in *"As you Like it"*, written in 1599.

In 1654 James Ussher (1581-1656) Archbishop of Armagh and Primate of all Ireland decided upon Sunday, October 23, 4004 B.C. as creation day. His date became part of the marginal notations in the authorized edition of the King James Bible printed in 1701. It came to be as accepted as if it had been handed down by the Prophets of Old. Ussher fine-tuned his calculation with biblical precision and wrote "notwithstanding the stay of the sun in the dayes of Joshua, and the going back of it in the dayes of Ezekiah." The distinguished rabbinical scholar, Dr. John Lightfoot (1602-1675) of Cambridge University even pronounced the very hour of creation as 9 a.m. Some quick addition of biblical begats shows that Noah's flood occurred 1646 years after the Creation, or at 2358 B.C.

Many creationists, embarrassed by so recent an origin of the Earth but adhering to biblical inerrancy, extend the beginning as from 6,000 to 10,000 years ago. This is 8,000 years plus or minus 2,000 — a remarkable uncertainty for so recent an event. In contrast, geologists date the earth as 4.55 plus or minus 2 percent billion years old — a hard fact obtained by several radiometric approaches. In the past three decades since geologists first announced their radiometric estimate of the earth's age as approximately 4.5 billion years, it has been confirmed and reconfirmed many times. There is thus a disagreement between the scientists and creationists by a factor of about one million, which is hardly trivial. There has been a written history for nearly 6,000 years, but nowhere is there any record of the dramatic events which would have occurred according to the creationists' time scale during this interval, such as the opening of the Atlantic Ocean or the collision of India with Asia to form the Himalayas. If creationists really believe that the Earth was created in 4004 B.C., they should propose a 6,000 year anniversary celebration in 1996. Such romantic ideas, conceived in the childhood of Western civilization have now been gently put aside by all except the fundamentalists. "When I was a child, I spake as a child, I understood as a child, I thought as a child: but when I became a man, I put away childish things." (1 Corinthians 13:11)

Adoption of the creationists dates requires the abandonment of essentially all modern

*No, I can't claim to have ever read the Bible, but I did read the
23rd Psalm — and I liked it.*

72

astronomy, much of modern physics, and most of the earth sciences. Much more than evolutionary biology is at stake. Three different methods provide an age for the universe of about 15 billion years, or 2.5 million times the 6,000 year age suggested by creationists. Fundamentalists disbelieve the consistency of radioactive decay assumed in using radiometric "clocks" to establish the earth's age as 4.5 billion years, but nuclear reactors depend upon this constancy. They would have to explain anew how these power-generating devices work. Creationists also attempt to explain away the evidence of an ancient earth and universe by assuming that the evidence itself was created. They propose that the light from distant stars was conveniently created in-transit to the earth. This implies a deceitful God. Most scientists have an abiding faith in the reasonableness of the world. If God doesn't want to play fair, scientists don't want to play.

I was heading north, through Bakersfield
Listening to gospel music on the colored radio station.
And the preacher said, "You know that the good Lord is always by your side."
And I was so pleased to be informed of this
That I ran 20 red lights in His honor
Thank you Jesus
Thank you Lord

---Mick Jagger, The Rolling Stones

As all biblical scholars agree, there are two versions of creation in the opening chapters of Genesis, the so-called P(priestly) and J(Jehovic) versions. The first verse of the modern bible (King James Version) reads: "In the beginning God created the heaven and the earth." But the earliest Hebrew text in the J version reads: "In the beginning *Elohim* created...." *Elohim* is the plural form of *Eloah* — the supreme being of the Jews. Hence a correct translation would be: "In the beginning the *gods* created heaven and earth." The early Jews were polytheistic and the idea of *one* God arose later.

When Mark Twain visited the Holy Land, a Christian zealot showed him the very clod of ground from which God created Adam. Said Twain: "It must be true, as no one has been able to prove anything different."

Sorrowing parents whose sons have been drafted or recalled for combat duty for the Korean War were told yesterday in St. Patrick's Cathedral by Monsignor William T. Greene that death in battle was a part of God's plan for populating the Kingdom of Heaven.---The New York Times, 9/11/50.

As for man he doesn't even consider himself an animal, which, considering the way he considers them, is probably, all things considered, the only considerate thing about him. --- Cleveland Amory

Anyone who ascribes to biblical inerrancy and infallibility is treading on a quagmire. It's a can of worms. And, once a can of worms is opened, a larger can is needed to re-can them.

A prayer has never been answered, is not answered, and never will be answered. --- Madeline Murray O'Hair, American Atheists

7

SALT IN THE OCEAN, ETC.: PROOFS OF AN ANCIENT EARTH

Geologists believe the earth to be very old. Nowadays, ancient geological events are best measured by resorting to radiometric "clocks" of which there are many. But an ancient earth was envisioned long before such clocks were discovered. A few examples of why the earth is considered old follow:

Salt in the Ocean. A minimum age for the earth can be estimated by the 3.5 percent salinity of the world's oceans. If we measure the amount of salt being added yearly to the oceans from the world's rivers, we find that it would take 330 million years to obtain the present salinity. This is just a *minimum* age as salt is also removed from the ocean during the formation of salt beds common in the geologic column.

Green River Lake Beds in Western U.S. In the Rocky Mountains, geologists have discovered the sediments of an ancient lake which existed 40 million years ago in the Eocene epoch. These beds are called the Green River oil shales and are an important future source for petroleum, a reserve equivalent to all the presently-known oil pools in the U.S.A. A prominent aspect of these shales are *varves* which are thin sedimentary couplets each representing a yearly cycle (summer and winter) of deposition. Geologists have counted some six million of these couplets indicating that this lake existed for six million years within the Eocene about 40 million years ago which itself is only a small fraction of geologic time.

Antarctic Ice Cap. The entire continent of Antarctica is covered with an ice cap about two miles thick. Under present rates of snowfall, glaciologists compute this accumulation required 10 million years. To build up such a thickness of ice in 6,000 years is inconceivable.

The Grand Canyon of the Colorado River. The mountains and plateaus of the world are deeply incised with canyons of which the Grand Canyon is the most majestic. Geologists reckon that 8 million years were needed for the river to cut its mile-deep canyon at present rates of erosion.

Bristlecone Pine. The oldest living things on earth are the bristlecone pines of the

western U.S.A. The age of trees can be readily established by tree rings which record annual cycles of growth. The bristlecone pine growth record, including associated dead stumps, has been carried back to 8,400 years. It would seem that these trees are older than the Garden of Eden.

The Sedimentary Record. The science of Historical Geology attempts to read the history of the earth from the sedimentary strata. These beds are said to be like the pages of a book, but with many missing and torn pages. In no single spot is the record complete without many interruptions. The Book of the Earth is not easy to decipher, but the composite sequence has a total thickness of about 150 kilometers. Based upon reasonable rates of sedimentation geologists a century ago figured the earth to be two billion years old. But much of the early sedimentary record has been eroded away and new methods based upon radiometric clocks show the earth to be 4.5 billion years old. More exactly geologist reckon the age of the earth to be 4.55 billion years plus or minus 2 percent. Fudging a bit on Bishop Ussher's figures, creationists commonly argue the earth to be 8,000 years plus or minus 25 percent. Wow!

8

ARK-EOLOGY AND THE GREAT FLOOD

— *Reprinted with permission, Bob Englehart,* Hartford Courant

A basic tenent of creationism is the reality of the Noachian Flood which supposedly inundated the entire earth to oceanic depths about 4,400 years ago or about 2400 B.C., accepting Archbishop Ussher's geneological timetable. Noah lived about 1,600 years after the earth's creation 6,000 years ago. The waters of the Great Flood overtopped Mt. Ararat by 10 cubits (15 feet) making the depth 16,915 (3 miles!) feet above modern sea level.

By the version of Whitcomb and Morris, chief ideologs of the creationist movement, in *The Genesis Flood*, the flood was turbulent and explains all the geologic, erosional, and sedimentary fossil record. Lasting a little more than a year, the surging waters scooped out enormous crevasses like the Grand Canyon. According to Henry Morris in his book *Biblical Cosmology and Modern Science:* "The main reason for insisting on the universal flood as a fact of history and as the primary vehicle for geological interpretation is that God's word plainly teaches it! No geological difficulties, real or imagined, can be allowed to take precedence over the clear statements and necessary inferences of Scripture." Remarkably a wholly different view is offered by another fundamentalist, D.A. Young. Although teaching in

Actually, there were three arks. The one with the dinosaurs and other extinct forms sank due to overloading. The one with marsupials was blown off course and landed in Australia.

a Bible college, he is a geologist and apparently finds it necessary to realistically relate to the record of the rocks. Constrained by this reality he describes in his recent book a *quiet* Noachian Flood in which the water rose and receded but with absolutely *no effect* on the earth's surficial features. Why can't these two bible "scientists" get their acts together?

Henry Morris suggests that during the Great Flood, the fauna under Noah's care were kept in torpor by "divinely-ordered genetic mutations experienced by the individuals selected for preservation in the Ark, equipping them with the capacities for migration and hibernation." (Inconsistently he argues elsewhere that evolution cannot happen because all mutations are deleterious). Such miracles are by definition violations of the laws of nature and, hence, beyond experimental scrutiny. Any theory which employs them loses its status as a science. Science is a unique attempt to explain the observable world on its own terms — that is, without supernatural events. In all history science has never resorted to supernatural or miraculous hypotheses to explain phenomena. Yet, for creationism, the Noachian Flood, with its miraculous rescue of animals, is not a minor theme but a key feature. Without it there is no creationist explanation for sedimentation, mountain building, great erosion, fossils, coal beds and glaciation. Everything depends on the flood.

The universal flood is part of all "scientific" creation models and is included in draft creationism legislation being advocated across the U.S.A. By its own canon, it is not scientific and consequently has no more business in the science classroom than a ghost story. Creationists are wedded to advancing a particular religious creed. The actual facts exist only to be explained away. As Henry Morris writes: "If we are to know anything about creation — when it was, what methods were used, in what order the events occurred, or anthing else we must depend *completely* on Divine Revelation." Those who accept this bizarre tale are rejecting knowledge and accepting faith — faith of that irrational variety expressed in the old quip of: "Believing in something you know is not true".

The creationists' textbook, *Biology: A Search for Order in Complexity,* explains the fossil record thusly: "...most fossil material was laid down by the flood in Noah's time. As the flood waters rose, less complex forms, being less able to escape, would be buried first. More complex and more mobile forms could move to higher grounds." This sorting by mobility and hydraulics is amusing enough for the record of animal fossils which are highly ordered from the simple to the highly complex. But consider the plants which are fixed in the soil. The fossil origins of flowering plants date back to about 120 million years, non-flowering seed plants (which include conifers) to about 350 millions years, spore-bearing plants (which include ferns) to about 400 million years, and multi-cellular green algae to about 600 million years. The fossil record of plants is highly ordered rather than jumbled.

Early catastrophists two centuries ago supposed that the thin rubbly veneer of unconsolidated soil overlying the bedrock of northern Europe and North America was laid down by the Biblical Flood. The supposed flood deposit was termed "diluvium" but never in their wildest dreams did they ever suppose that the underlying lithified sedimentary strata were ever in any way connected with the Noachian Deluge. This surficial diluvium was recognized about 1850 as glacial till deposited by the extensive continental glaciers of the Ice Age. The early catastrophists have been outdone by modern creationists who ascribe the *entire* sedimentary record and all of its contained fossils to the flood.

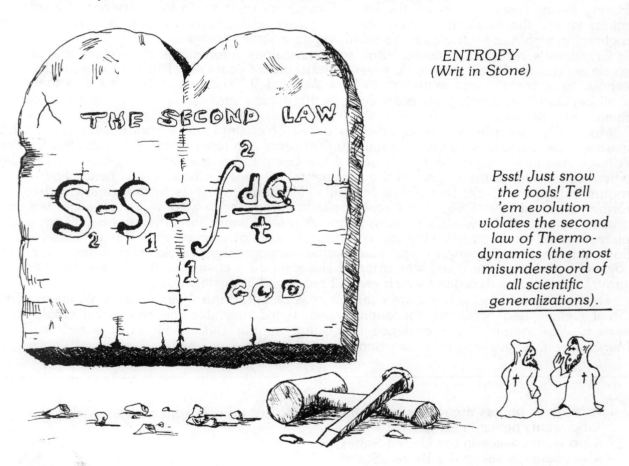

ENTROPY
(Writ in Stone)

Psst! Just snow the fools! Tell 'em evolution violates the second law of Thermodynamics (the most misunderstoord of all scientific generalizations).

The creationists also explain coal beds by the flood. Supposedly the world's forests were uprooted, deposited as vegetative mats and quickly converted to coal. But if all the plants on earth today were suddenly converted to coal, their total mass would only be equal to one percent of the known coal reserves. In the Illinois Basin alone, there are 80 coal beds which would seem to require *eighty* Great Floods for their formation. All ancient coal beds are composed of plants which are no longer found on the face of the earth — for example, fossils of flowering plants are not present. To ascribe coal beds to the Noachian Flood is bizarre in the extreme.

It is a matter of fundamentalists first principles that a pair of *every* "kind" were loaded onto the Ark. The Bible says so! The literal inerrancy of the Bible is so ingrained in the "true believers" that one speaker at a recent Seventh Day Adventist Congress remarked: "Even if the Bible recorded that *Jonah* swallowed the whale, I would still believe it." So the dinosaurs must have been included on the voyage. Apparently God could not predict the weather any better than the *Old Farmer's Almanac* because, if He realized that the dinosaurs were all going to be killed off anyway by the post-flood climate deterioration, as is the standard creationist claim, He should have ordered Noah to leave them behind.

Creationists, embarrassed by a three-mile-deep flood, commonly claim that mountains only formed after the Deluge or that Mt. Ararat was not as high as now, but such apologetics do not wash. The Bible clearly records in Genesis 8:5 that the waters withdrew to reveal the mountains. Mt. Ararat is a volcanic mountain which in turn rests upon a thick sedimentary sequence. In the creationists view the sediments had to be first laid down by the flood waters and the volcanic edifice later extruded but before the Deluge ended — a wild scenario! And to compound the problem, Why are there no marine fossils atop Ararat?

The mythology of a Great Flood is found not only in the Bible but in many other early cultures. Scholars believe that the Biblical account is derived from an earlier Babylonian myth. Does the worldwide extent of their legend reinforce the reality of the Noachian Flood? Not really. Accounts of "the sky is falling" are even more universal. It fell many times before Henny Penny rushed off to tell the king of imminent disaster. In the workings of a primitive mind, where the vault of heaven rests on pillars, collapse of the sky is a recurring and frightening nightmare. One culture's mythology is another's religion.

Creationists resort to catastrophism and miraculous happenings to explain the geologic scene as wrought by an earth only several thousands of years old. But the Bible mocks them, espousing uniformity and actualism in Ecclesiastes 1:9 "That which hath been is that which shall be; and that which hath been done is that which shall be done; and there is no new thing under the sun."

Modern geomorphology *does* offer an excellent example of a catastrophic flood which washed over eastern Washington about 20,000 years ago toward the end of the last Ice Age. A huge lake in Montana the size of one of the Great Lakes suddenly emptied in a few days when an ice dam at the margin of the continental ice sheet collapsed. Old beach lines on the mountain slopes, 1,000 feet above Missoula, Montana, attest as to the great depth of this former dammed lake. Called the Great Spokane Flood, the flow for a few days was ten times greater than all of the world's modern rivers. A wall of water surged across 8,000 sq. km. of plateau land, vastly overflowing the confines of existing river valleys. This cataclysmic flash flood left an indelible imprint, peculiar braided topography, visible even from space. The loessial (wind deposited) soil was stripped like icing off a cake. Enormous boulder trains and gravel ripples were deposited which are still preserved in pristine condition.

The Spokane Flood is a unique example of a recent, natural but cataclysmic event. If the Great Deluge had occurred, the entire world would resemble the *channeled scablands* of eastern Washington. Such evidence is lacking, so the Biblical Flood is a fiction! Baron Munchausen, where are you now when we need you?

The religious papers are rather interesting reading just now. It appears that
   God wants peace in Britain
   God wants peace in the United States
   God wants peace in the Balkan States
   God wants peace in France
   God wants peace all over the world, but
   Hitler won't let him have it.---*The Freethinker, 1942*

When uncertain
When in doubt
Run in circles
Scream and shout

Whoever has theologian's blood in his veins has a wrong and dishonest attitude toward all things...What a theologian feels to be true necessarily must be false. This is almost a criterion for truth...---Fredriche Nietzsche (1844-1900)

9

NOAH: ASTRO-NUTS AND ARK-O-NAUTS

In the past decade, a few hundred religious zealots have scaled Mt. Ararat in search of Noah's Ark. And why not? The supposedly inerrant Bible in Genesis (chapters 6-10) tells us that the Ark landed atop the three-mile high dormant volcano. Never mind that the great flood story was filched from the older "Tale of Utnaphishtim", a part of the Babylonian sacred *Gilgamesh Epic* written in cuneiform about 2,000 B.C. The Babylonian myth contains the identical storyline of the Genesis account including such details as sending out a raven and a dove to search for land. Flood legends are widespread among primitive tribes which the creationists claim reinforces the reality of the Noachian Flood. But another legendary catastrophe is even more prevalent — this is that the sky is about to fall. And why not?, a crystalline dome or firmament was supposed to separate the waters above the earth from those below. The ancients thought they could even see the waters on high because the sky is blue. What better proof is needed?

The usual creationist apologetic is that Mt. Ararat (17,000 feet) was not so high as now at the time of the flood. But, remember, Ararat is a volcano and the ark supposedly landed near the top. So the volcano must have erupted and grown in a matter of a few weeks while the flood waters were receding because you can't dock an ark on flowing lava. And Ararat could not have existed at all before the flood because this volcano rests on top of some 7,000 feet of sediment which is a flood deposit by the creationist scenario.

Astronauts of the U.S.A. space program are presumably expected to be reasonably intelligent as well as having flying skills. But among these was James Irwin, whose life work now seems to be searching for Noah's Ark. At least he has led four Ark-eological expeditions to Mt. Ararat. How incredibly naive! Even to get to the moon, he had to penetrate the supposedly crystalline firmament and the "waters above the earth" as described in Genesis. On his flight to the moon (Apollo 15) Irwin recovered an unusual whitish rock which came to be known as the Genesis rock — a piece of the early surface of the moon. Studies by scientists revealed that this specimen is, indeed, among the oldest lunar rocks. Its age is close to that of our satellite — 4.55 billion years. Yet, ascribing to the inerrancy of the Bible, Irwin presumably believes this genesis rock to be only 6,000 years old, having been created in 4004 B.C.

Not only did Noah have to collect pairs of all the two million species in the animal and plant kingdoms, but also all of the species in three other great kingdoms of life: the fungi; protists, the single celled protozoans; and the monera, the bacteria and viruses. By creationist's rules they cannot have evolved any more than the plants and animals. By the modern germ theory of diseases, the microbes are living entities — namely protozoans, viruses and bacteria many of which can only survive in human hosts. We must envision Noah and his crew being infected with tapeworms, malaria, syphilus, smallpox, and AIDS to name a few.

An apologetic resorted to by creationists is that God placed the animals on the ark in a state of suspended animation. But Genesis tells us that the animals came off in *families*, —i.e. parents plus offspring. So they were actively procreating aboard the ark and not in a state of stupor. Noah captained the first known Love Boat. (Based on an article by Frank Zindler)

Father Charles Curran of the Catholic University got himself into holy hot water in August 1986. For his stance on the ethics of sexual morality, the theologian was zinged by the Cardinal Joseph Ratzinger, head of the Vatican's Congregation for the Doctrine of the Faith, who revoked Curran's right to teach theology. Curran believes that the church should ease it's ban on such things as remarriage after divorce. He defended his views on the grounds of intellectual dissent and that these were not contravening those infallible dogmas which are divinely protected from error—for example, the bodily assumption of Mary into Heaven which everyone(?) knows to be true. But it seems that his karma was running over the churches dogma! At least Joe Ratzinger thought so and charged Curran with "thinking without a license."

10

PALUXY MANTRACKS IN TEXAS: THE FOSSILS SAY "NO!"

Since 1939, excellent fossil trackways of dinosaurs have been known from an area of northcentral Texas 50 miles southwest of Dallas along the Paluxy River near the town of Glen Rose. The dinosaur tracks are found preserved in the Glen Rose limestone of middle Cretaceous age about 100 million years old — the heyday of these giant reptiles.

Unlike geologists who see order down the long corridor of time recorded in the sedimentary layers, creationists are compelled by the Book of Genesis to insist ("the evidence be damned") on a young and chaotically jumbled sequence of rocks laid down by the Noachian Flood. Accordingly, creationists claim some of these tracks are human footprints rather than eroded dinosaur tracks, erosion features, or forgeries. Even the creationist Barney Newfeld regarded the alleged human prints as made not by the foot of man, but by the hand of man. Local townspeople admit to carving examples and selling them to tourists. One large imprint, the Big Foot track, is 16 inches long and is as perfect a giant's footprint as was ever sold at a county fair. Most of the so-called human tracks are actually the toe prints of a three-toed carnivorous dinosaur in which the heel was not implanted and preserved. The stride is usually six feet or exactly that of the dinosaur. Creationists never hesitate to enhance the human-like shape of these prints by painting them with oil or adjusting the lighting before photographing them.

The great size of the Paluxy tracks according to creationists, were created by giants who lived in those early days as written in the Bible. Of course biblical patriarchs are said to have lived to ripe old ages of more than 900 years, for example, Noah and Methusalah. But great age does not mean giantism as mammals attain their adult size early in life and grow no larger — unlike fish, amphibians and reptiles which grow throughout their lifespan.

Actually, these footprints of terrestrial animals on bedding planes are strong evidence against the Noachian flood. After all, the flood waters must have receded to expose these sediments, so that these animals could tippy-toe across the mud flats before the waters returned and covered them with more mud. Where were these animals living before they made their tracks? They must have been on some dry land nearby but the Bible records that the earth was completely inundated. Elsewhere so-called hand tracks are known. But these are actually the footprint of a dinosaur known as *Cliotherium* which literally means the hand-reptile. These trackways cannot be the imprint of a human hand because some of them reveal scales and the "thumb" is on the wrong side of the hand.

11

OFF THE TRACK: CREATIONISTS RETRACT "MANPRINTS" CLAIM AT PALUXY IN TEXAS

For 30 years creationists interested in debunking evolution have travelled to Paluxy Creek near Glen Rose, Texas, to claim that giant "mantracks" co-exist with three-toed dinosaur trackways in the 70 million-year-old Glen Rose limestone. To creationists, the rationale was simple: Man plus dinosaur tracks in the same stratum proved coexistence of man and dinosaur, supporting their belief that the world was created in six days, no more than ten thousand years ago. Paleontologists have always argued that all of the tracks are modified or imperfect dinosaur footprints which simply have undergone initial slumping, sliding, or later erosion. Indeed, they do appear somewhat human-like but the 15-inch footpad and the six foot stride would have required a giant. But a recent detailed, and elegant study by Glen Kuban, an amateur paleontologist, has convinced even the leading creationists of the Institute for Creation Research (ICR) in San Diego that there are *no* human footprints. John Morris of ICR and son of the leading creationist Henry Morris, head of ICR admitted that the Kuban findings were a bit embarrassing. "It looks bad," Morris said, "It looks like we made a mistake. And it looks like we better stop using the tracks."

The clinching evidence found by Kuban was discoloration at the top of each footprint which clearly showed the toeprints of a three-toed dinosaur. These did not show up at the time of the initial excavation, but a few years of weathering and oxidation brought them to light like a latent image on a piece of exposed film.

In 1980, John Morris wrote a book entitled, *Tracking Those Incredible Dinosaurs...and the People Who Knew Them* which became a best seller in creationist circles. Earlier, in 1972, a creationist documentary film was produced called *Footprints in Stone* and distributed by Films for Christ. Both the book and the film have been withdrawn from circulation. Perhaps a better title for the book would have been *Tracking Those Incredible Creationists* and, for the film, *Footprints in the Mind.*

Last words of the Prophet Zachariah: "One man's Mede is another man's Persian."

12

LIGHTNING: ACT OF GOD OR NATURE?

Thunder and lightning were considered to be token's of God's displeasure so that prayer was regarded as a sufficient antidote. Saint Thomas Aquinas wrote in his *Summa Theologica* that: "Rain and winds, and whatsoever occurs by local impulse alone, can be caused by demons. It is a dogma of faith that demons can produce winds, storms, and rains of fire from heaven." In sixteenth century England, church towers were protected by the local bishop who "sayd certen Psalmes and with holy oyle draweth the signe of the crosse, and prayeth God, that whan they shall rynge or sounde the bell, all the deceiptes of the devyll may vanyshe away, hayle, thondryng, ligthening, wynds, and tempestes, and all the untemperate weathers may be aswaged." Such prayers were of little avail and, in Germany, within a span of three decades some 400 church towers were damaged by lightning and 120 bell ringers killed. In one church a bolt of lightning struck the tower and melted the bell, electrocuted the priest, deprived a parishoner of her sensibilities and destroyed a painting of the Savior.

Church towers, being the highest structures in a village, are commonly struck by lightning, while brothels and saloons next door escape untouched. Although Benjamin Franklin discovered the nature of lightning and invented the lightning rod in 1752, its use was largely rejected for many years. Nowadays lightning rods protect all churches and control "the artillery of heaven". Once again the supremacy of science is established by recognizing that the enemy is nature rather than Satan.

13

VALUE OF PI AND OTHER FOIBLES

The Value of Pi. 1st Kings 7:23 states that an altar font (the Molten Sea) in Solomon's Temple built about 1,000 B.C. was ten cubits across and thirty cubits around. This is inaccurate as it provides a value of 3.00 for pi rather than 3.1416. There is no evidence, as apologists suggest, that the Hebrew author was "speaking in an approximate way." The Bible is either perfect, i.e., inerrant, or it isn't. There is no in-between. To admit a calculation is only "approximate" is to admit that the calculation is false and the Bible is errant.

At the end of the last century, a legislator in Indiana, exasperated by the calculations of a mathematician who carried pi to 400 decimal places, and still could not achieve a rational number, proposed a law that would make pi equal to exactly 3.0.

Mathematical Proof of God's Existence. Dennis Didirot (1713-1784), a French mathematician and philosopher, did much to bring Europe out of its dark slumber. In 1773, he visited the Empress Catherine of Russia to discuss the sale of his extensive library for 1,000 pounds of silver. Aware that he was a "fallen-away" Jesuit and free-thinker, the Queen laid a trap for him at the court in St. Petersburg. At her behest the Russian mathematician, Leonard Euler challenged Didirot with a mathematical "proof" of God's existence. Said Euler with ringing conviction: "Sir, $A + B^\circ/Z = X$. Therefore, God exists! Reply." Caught off guard, Didirot offered only a cogent comment somewhat lacking in decorum. Muttered he, *"Merde."*

Heaven Hotter Than Hell. Heaven may be a nice place to go when you die, but you would not want to live there. Why? Because it is hotter than Hell if we accept the Bible as scientifically inerrant. The authority is Isaiah 30:26 which reads concerning Heaven, "Moreover the light of the moon shall be as the light of the sun and the light of the sun shall be sevenfold, as the light of seven days." Accordingly Heaven receives from the moon as much radiation as we do from the sun and, additionally, 49 (7x7) times as much radiation from the heavenly sun as we do from our sun. From these data we can obtain the temperature of Heaven using the Stefan-Boltzmann fourth-power law for radiation which computes to be 525 degrees centigrade.

The exact temperature of Hell cannot be computed from biblical data except that it must be less than 445° C which is the temperature at which brimstone or sulphur evaporates from a liquid to a gaseous phase. Revelations 21:8 tells us: "But the fearful, and unbelieving...shall have their part in the lake which burneth with fire and brimstone." A lake of molten brimstone requires that the temperature be below the boiling point of sulphur (445° C) because above this point only a sulphurous vapor would be present.

The temperature of Heaven is thus 525° C and that of Hell less than 445° C; *ergo* Heaven is hotter than Hell. Interestingly, the surface of Venus (425° C) is the only place among the terrestrial planets where we find a heaven-like temperature — and clouds of sulfuric acid.

As The World Turns. A recent bit of creation science nonsense has been generated by Walter T. Brown, head of the Midwest Center of the Institute for Creation Research. Aware that a leap second is added to astronomical clocks every few years, he jumped to the conclusion that the earth is slowing at an alarming rate. Needing more time to complete a revolution and going into history, the earth would have been spinning at an impossibly high rate if as old as geologists believe. But the leap-second is roughly on a par with the leap year when we add one day every fourth year. This does not mean that the year is growing longer, but only that the earth does not circle the sun in exactly an equal number of days each year. The addition of a leap second is not quite the same but it in no way indicates that the earth is slowing down at a rapid rate. Instead, it confirms the geophysicists's view that the earth is a few billion years old. (Walter Brown has recently admitted his calculations were wrong.)

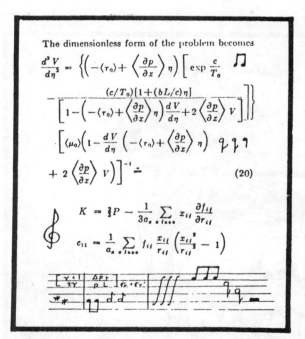

Mathetical proof of the existence of God — orchestrated for oboe, flute, and harp

The religion-builders have so distorted and deformed the doctrines of Jesus, so muffled them in mysticisms, fancies and falsehoods, and have caricatured them into forms so monstrous and inconceivable, as to shock reasonable thinkers.

—Thomas Jefferson

New York, March 5 (UP) — Wilbur G. Volviva, chief of Zion City, Ill., (a religious community), who has just finished a trip around the world, has pronounced himself more convinced than ever that this earth is a flat disk, not a globe. —News item, 1986.

Comedian George Carlin has observed that there are some words that just don't seem to go together. He gives as examples the terms *jumbo shrimp* and *military intelligence*. I think that there can be little doubt that top honors for such contradictions-in-terms should go to *scientific creationism.* — Leon Albert, anthropologist.

My own mind is my own church.

The church is a human invention set up to terrify and enslave mankind and to monopolize power and profit.

The Jews prove the falsity of Jesus and Christianity by producing the people who say it is not true.

14

THEOPHYSICS AND OTHER THEOSCIENCE

The Earth Is Flat. Teachers shouldn't try to dissuade pupils who want to believe the world is flat, Arizona Gov. Evan Meecham's education advisor said recently (Feb. 1987).

"If that student wants to say the world is flat, the teacher doesn't have the right to try to prove otherwise," former Rep. Jim Cooper, a Mesa Republican, told the House Education Committee.

Cooper, the committee's former chairman, was testifying on House Bill 2095, which would require schools that teach evolution to present it as a theory rather than fact. No vote was taken on the bill.

Cooper said teachers should not try to talk pupils out of beliefs they acquire at home. If a pupil believes in biblical creationism rather than evolution as the origin of humans, the teacher should not dispute it, he said.

Rep. Peter Goudinoff, D-Tucson, asked Cooper what should happen if a pupil told his geography teacher that his parents said the world is flat.

"The schools don't have any business telling people what to believe," Cooper replied.

Goudinoff asked whether a teacher would have to give a passing grade to a pupil who wrote on an exam that the world is flat, adding, "How do you maintain academic standards?"

Cooper answered, "I don't worry about that part of it."

State Superintendent of Public Instruction C. Diane Bishop appeared taken aback when told of Cooper's remarks. --- The Arizona Republic, newspaper article

—Reprinted with permission, by Benson of the Arizona Republic

The Earth Is Hollow. After a creation seminar on October 24, 1986, Henry Morris, head of the Institution for Creation Research, was asked about the bottomless pit refered to in the Book of Revelation, Chap. 9:1-11. He explained the reference as follows:

"How can there be a bottomless pit? Well, very simple. Always, whenever Hades or Sheol is referred to in the Bible, it's always down in the earth, the depths of the earth. So right there in the center of the earth, apparently, there's a great opening that we can't really deal with in terms of our seismic instruments or other instrumentation. But it apparently is there. You can take the Bible to mean what it says, and I think we have to do that. And of course, since it is at the center of the earth, every boundary has a ceiling. It doesn't have a bottom; it's a bottomless pit." ... from Creation - Evolution Newsletter, 1986.

If the Creationists Win. If the creationists win, and they well might, do not think that biology with its foundation on Darwinian evolution would be the only casualty. All liberal arts and sciences will be devastated. Here are a few examples of possible school curricula under creationist direction:

Creation astronomy: The craters on the moon resulted from a great battle between God and Satan's rebel angels. (Henry Morris — Leading creationist.)

Creation linguistics: Languages did not evolve over the past 50,000 years but were instantly created with the fall of the Tower of Babel by God's anger as a punishment for human pride.

Creation geology: The earth was created about 6,000 years ago (Oct. 23 at 0900 hours, 4,004 B.C.) and was inundated by a world wide Noachian Flood three miles deep, about 2,300 B.C.

Creation history: All races of man (black, white, yellow, and brown) and all cultures were derived from the eight survivors in Noah's Ark. And these eight have propagated to the over five billion persons alive today.

Creation psychology: Moral values are absolute, inflexible, and based on concepts of sin, guilt, and a hierarchical spiral descending from God to man to woman to child.

Creation Atmospherics: Televangelist Pat Robertson on his 700 Club recently offered the following: "I think the sky is blue because it's a shift from black through purple to blue, and it has to do with where the light is. You know, the farther we get into darkness, and there's a shifting of color of light into the blueness, and I think as you go farther and farther away from the reflected light we have from the sun or the light that's bouncing off this earth, uh, the darker it gets ... I think if you look at the color scale, you start at black, move it through purple, move it on out, it's the shifting of color. We mentioned before about the stars singing [it's in the Bible], and that's one of the effects of the shift of color."

Well, Robertson really blew that one. He should have stuck with the Bible. In biblical cosmology (see Genesis) the sky is blue because water is blue. If you look upward you see through the firmament, the transparent crystalline dome of the sky, which separates the waters above the earth from those below. So, of course, you see the blue of the waters above the firmament. Where do you think rain comes from, dumb-dumb?

Creation taxonomy: Some 6,000 years ago, the Bible tells us in Gen. 2:19 that "out of the ground the Lord God formed every living beast of the field and every fowl of the air, and brought them unto Adam to see what they would call them: and whatsoever Adam called every living creature, that was the name thereof."[1]

---

[1]Ref: James, K. (1635) The Holy Bible: The Gideon International, Motel 6, Tempe AZ, 942 pp. (free)

But the Bible gives no clue as to what Adam *actually* called them or their *hierarchial* ranking. Man would be at the top, naturally, and man's "best friend," the dog, probably second and so on.[1] Well, that is the major clue right there according to Pastor Thaddeus Crabtree.

Remember, he says, all lower animals share, with *Homo sapiens,* the ability to produce spondees. These, unlike the more advance trochees, are bisyllabic words with equal emphases on each syllable. Speech therapists and language pathologists have long recognized the value of such vocalizations in their diagnostic evaluations. Examples of spondees are *dingbat, icebox,* and *oddball.*

Placing spondees in an hierarchical sequence proved, says Crabtree, to be as simple as the ABC's, totally avoiding heuristic rules and non-parametric parameters. Adam simply placed them alphabetically; himself first (A is really for Adam and not apple) and then *arf arf,* his best friend, second. Adam would obviously then use onomatopoeia in naming animals. Only after the fall of the Tower of Babel by God's angels was humankind cursed to speak in tongues. *Arf arf* then became *hund* (German), *chien* (French), *dog* English), etc. (There remains the possibility that there were micro-evolutionary changes from *woof woof* to *bow bow* from the originally created *arf arf.*) With this simplistic beginning it has been possible to retrieve the names of the animals as coined by Adam and place them in hierarchical sequence, as this was alphabetical.

The fundamentalists are right in objecting to contra-Bible textbooks which claim that languages slowly evolved over a long period of time. Adam's listing follows:

Sample Data Table — Hierarchical Levels [2]

Highest Level Species	Spondee (Adam's Name)
Man	Adam
Dog	Arf-Arf
Sheep	Baa-Baa
Chicken	Cluck-Cluck
Frog	Gribbet
Jackass	Hee-Haw
Cat	Meow
Pig	Oink-Oink
Duck	Quack-quack
Owl	Who-Who
Lowest Level	

[1]This, of course, would be devolution (or devil-evolution), a downward spiral of increasing entropy — consistent with the second law of thermodynamics.

[2]There are many words, frequently used in theological discourses, for which there is no agreed upon meaning, and, perhaps, no meaning. These include heuristic, parameter, and hierarchical. But they are so fraught with conceivable import that they should be used as often as possible.

(Adapted from Gerald S. Golden)

Fundamentalists dismiss members of mainstream religions as not being "true" Christians. And in a parallel exercise in word magic they hold that evolutionists are not teaching "true" science. Then, they argue, that creation "science" has validity simply because some of its advocates have degrees in science fields. But degrees do not transform one's religious convictions into scientific propositions.

The creationists dismiss the idea that a monkey or an ass can be transformed into a man although they must be familiar with the reverse process.---Robert Millikan (1868-1953)

15

GLOSSARY

Bible: A classic tome of delightful whimsy written two to three thousand years ago somewhere west of Eden by half-civilized Hebrews — and some miscellaneous Shebrews as well. The opus is a compendium garbed in contorted convolutions, puerile platitudes, improbable parables, and archaic anachronisms, told and re-told in double re-entry flashback. Much of the text was passed along by word of mouth or voice-over. But owing to the total recall of these early near-savages, the sage words of the prophets were preserved verbatim, without embellishment or exaggeration. And in those days nobody lied. It was the first of the genre which depicts harlots as heroines and women as weak, tempting or irrelevant. The book achieved fame through the heroic megabuck films of Cecil B. Schemiel featuring rape, riot and revolution, with Robert Carizzma in the starring role. Being inerrant, inspired, infallible, and impossible, everyone now agrees that the Bible is the best guide to how we should live our lives.

Botany: The science of vegetables as opposed to animals and minerals. Special interest pertains to flowering plants which Man in his vanity, believes God created for our pleasure, but which were actually evolved to attract insects and promote effective cross-fertilization.

Cryptozoology: The study of Bigfoot, Paluxy Man, the Loch Ness Monster, the Abominable Snowman (Yetti) and other things that go bump in the night. Man is a very small thing, and the night is large and full of wonders.

Deluge: An impressive first exeriment in baptism which washed away the sinners as well as the sins of this world.

Eliptical Writing: Writing which equal sense, or lack thereof, when read forward or backward — or possibly sideways. A classical example is found in the tortured and perplexing writings of Mary Baker Eddy (1821-1910), the founder of *Christian Science* in which only the spirit world is real. Her basic propositions were:

God is all in all,
God is good, good is mind
God spirit being all, Nothing is matter

These basic axioms Mary Baker Eddy observed may be equally understood if read backwards. This, she believed, mathematically proved their perfection and exact correspondence with ultimate truth. Hence:

All in all is God
Mind is good, good is God
Matter is nothing, all being spirit God

The philosophy of religionists is succinct — children should be exposed only to a rigid set of ideas, to a fixed set of beliefs and facts consistent with the censors' view of history.

❊❊❊

Miracles, like UFO's, usually appear to those most inclined to see them. We tend to see what we are looking for.

❊❊❊

"...and Jesus, on your Second Coming, don't hang around with all those men so much. It gives some people the wrong impression." --- a prayer

❊❊❊

No one ever went broke underestimating the intelligence of the American public. If P.T. Barnum were alive today he would be an evangelist.

❊❊❊

Where's the beef? In my thirty-five years of investigating miracles, I have found a great deal of baloney, but precious little beef. --- A. Aaron Aardvark

Evangelist: A bearer of glad tidings insuring us of salvation while our enemies roast to a nut-brown discomfort in hell. --- A. Bierce

God:
1. The Supreme Being; the eternal and infinite Spirit, Creator and Sovereign of the universe. --- Webster's Dictionary
2. A being of more than human attributes and powers; a deity, especially a male deity. --- Webster's Dictionary
3. Old-Man-in-the-Sky. --- Buonarroti Michalengelo
4. Nature. --- Benedict Spinoza and Albert Einstein
5. Not supernatural but ultranatural. Can only be defined in terms of concepts yet to be discovered. --- Nobel Price
6. A Santa Claus for adults. --- A. Aaron Aardvark
7. Hydrogen. --- the astronomers' characterization
8. Eleventh dimensional De Sitter space. --- cosmologists' characterization
9. The great "I Am", all knowing, all seeing, all acting, all wise; all loving and eternal. Principal, mind, soul, spirit, life, truth, love, overall and all. --- Mary Baker Eddy. (If you are a mite confused by this definition, you are not alone.

Summary: If you are asked if you believe in God, the most confusing answer you can give is to say, "Yes."

Glossalalia: The gift of tongues. Pious prattle from a pulpit. To babble unintelligibly with intent to bamboozle. To talk while saying nothing — and vice versa. To listen only while talking. Commonly practiced by evangelists who, generally speaking, are generally speaking.

Heretic: A member of the clergy who has agreed, with bad grace, to differ.

Hyperbole: A statement so extravagent that it almost rings true. Example: "Jesus of Nazareth was the greatest scientist to ever trod the globe." (Mary Baker Eddy) A converse statement is: "The apparition of Karl Marx on earth was the Second Coming of the Messiah." --- Ichabod Balderdash

Hear no evolution,   speak no evolution,   see no evolution.

Infidel: A term of reproach which Christians and Muslims, in their modesty, agree to apply to each other.

Kaaba Stone: A large stone, said to be a meteorite, worshipped by Muslims at the sacred Kaaba temple in Mecca. The stone was hurled by the Archangel Gabriel at the Patriarch Abraham who asked for bread.

Metaphysics: A dash of the supernatural added to physics as offered by a guru while contemplating his own navel.

Millennium: The period of ten centuries after the return of Christ in 1996 when the lid is screwed down with all evangelists on the underside. --- A. Bierce

Morality: The theory that every human act must be right or wrong. --- H.L. Menken

Plain: A place in Spain where the rain falls mainly. In England, by contrast, the rain falls everywhere. The rain, it rained on the just / And on the unjust fella / But mostly on the just because / The unjust hath the just's umbrella.

Priest: A salaried urban witch doctor.

Prophet: One who navigates the sea of knowledge without the charts of science or the compass of education and ends always by discovering ultimate truths which somehow eluded the wisdom of the ages.

Robert's Law: Expect a miracle, nature is usually wrong!

Saint George: A saint renowned for slaying a fire-belching dragon, or, perhaps, a dragon fly. He is not to be confused with Jack the Giant Killer who dispatched seven in one blow, — flies, that is. Nor with William Jennings Bryan who belched firey platitudes.

When Adam day by day;
Woke up in Paradise;
He always used to say;
"Oh, this is very nice."

But Eve from scenes of bliss;
Transported him for life;
The more I think of this;
The more I beat my wife.

A.E. Housman

Many good men believed the strange fables of Christianity and have lived very good lives — for credulity is not a crime.

Which books to include in the Bible, was decided by a vote of the church. The Apocrypha were left out.

Prophets and divines are fond of puzzling one another.

It is a shame to call the paltry stories of the Bible, the word of God. They are historical, anecdotal poetry.

Shaman: An annoited thaumaturgist dating from the Primitive Period who, in cahoots with the Holy Spirit, makes valuable objects disappear — usually into his own pocket. Formerly written, sham-man.

Thunderstones: Human artifacts such as spearheads unearthed in Medieval Europe and dismissed as "thunderstones" — weapons hurled by Gods and miscellaneous supernatural personages. In those days the idea of pre-Adam stone-age men was an unthinkable heresy. At the end of the 16th century Michael Mercati tried to prove that these artifacts were the weapons and implements of primitive men. Not so, claimed the learned Tollius who in 1649 informed the world that these fashioned stones were "generated in the sky by a fulgurous exhalation conglobed in a cloud by the circumposed humor".

Trinity: Among the primitive tribes of New Guinea, three gods with one head. For Christian, a three-headed God.

Triskaidekaphobia: Fear of the number 13 and especially when Friday falls on the thirteenth day of the month. In 1986 triskaidekaphobics had to hide under the be four times (February, March, June, and November). The fear stems from Adam and Eve falling from grace on Friday; the Noachian Flood starting on Friday; the temple of Soloman tumbling on Friday; and Jesus being crucified on Friday; and the Rt. Reverend Eziah Piddlestone being kicked to death in 1878 by a bunny rabbit on Friday. But one must not get completely unraveled for as Pogo, the philosophizing comic strip possum once said: "Lucky us. Friday the thirteenth comes on Tuesday this month".

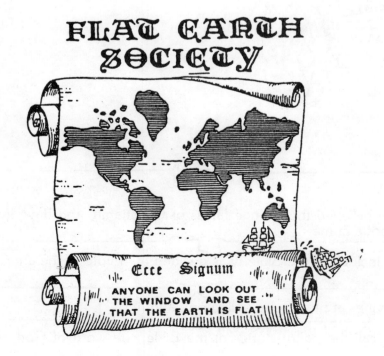

FLAT EARTH SOCIETY

Ecce Signum

ANYONE CAN LOOK OUT THE WINDOW AND SEE THAT THE EARTH IS FLAT

PART 4
EVOLUTION AND CREATIONISM

TWO FAVORITE PLEASANTRIES
OF RONALD REAGAN

An old fellow who had a piece of barren land got ambitious and went to work clearing the brush, hauling away the rocks, cultivating the soil and planting. Finally, he had a beautiful garden spot there. He was so proud that one Sunday morning he asked a minister to come by after church services and see what he had done. The minister was impressed. "I've never seen corn so tall. My, how the Lord blessed this land. Look at those melons. Praise the Lord." And he went on like that. Well, the old boy was getting fidgety as the minister kept giving the Lord credit and he finally interrupted, "Reverend, I wish you could have seen this place when the Lord was doing it by himself."

A young fellow of Irish heritage was in court suing for $4 million. He was bandaged from head to toe and said he couldn't move a muscle as a result of an accident. He won the suit. The lawyers for the insurance company went over to him and said, "You're never going to enjoy a penny of that money. We know you're faking and we're going to follow you 24 hours a day. The first time you make a move, we'll have you." The lad said, "Will you now? Well, let me tell you what's going to happen to me. They're taking me out of here on a stretcher. Downstairs they're putting me in an ambulance which is taking me straight to Kennedy Airport. Then they're putting me on a plane that's going to Paris, France. In Paris, they're putting me in another ambulance which is taking me to the Shrine of Lourdes. And there, you will see the greatest miracle you ever saw."

1

EVOLUTION AND THE MAINSTREAM CHURCHES

The best kept secret of Christianity is that the mainstream churches have no problem in accommodating their theology with evolution and other findings of science. Clergy of the Catholic, Methodist and Episcopal churches have been particularly outspoken in their support of evolution. Pope John Paul II in an address to members of the Pontifical Academy of Sciences in 1981 said: "The Bible itself speaks to us of the origin of the universe and its make-up not in order to provide us with a scientific treatise, but in order to state the correct relationships of man with God and the Universe."

The Episcopal Church in a recent tri-annual meeting in New Orleans soundly condemned creationism and passed a resolution opposing its teaching in public schools. Many persons would be surprised to learn that even the fundamentalist Mormon Church has no opposition to evolution. A 1956 letter by then President and Prophet David O. McKay stated that the Mormon Church officially takes a neutral position on evolution even though some of its prominent members oppose it.

Nothing has so infuriated the aberrant fringe of Christianity as the concept of evolution. Since 1860 fundamentalists have incessantly waged war against Darwinism. Actually, evolution in no way necessarily contradicts the general Christian belief in an all-powerful God. It is true that evolution also fails to support many biblical verities and thus might be thought to be insufficiently holy. Evangelists believe that fundamentalism is the only alternative to godless secularism. Those who believe in evolution and the common ancestry of primates and humans cannot believe in God. All religions which have accommodated their theology to scientific knowledge are thereby branded as heretical.

J. FALWELL HIGH SCHOOL

NAME: Johnny Numbskull

GRADE: 10TH

1	8:20	Prayer	Robertson	166
2	8:30	Band	Sousa	213
3	9:30	Scientific Creationism	Morris	101
4	10:30	Fun and Games	Gish	Gym
5	11:30	God, Country and the U.S. Marines	Haig	132
6	12:30	Lunch	Swaggert	117
7	1:30	Bible Studies	Le Haye	202
8	2:30	Virtue	Roberts	Lib.
opt.	3:30	Bible Club		

Indoctrination or education?
Why Johnny can't read, spell or think.

I believe that when one is dead, one is dead for a very long time.---Jean Perrier, biologist

Truth is the poison of religion. When it is discovered religion dies. Truth is the food of science. When it is ingested, science evolves.

The biblical account of creation and belief in God are compatible with the theory of evolution. "[Belief in] evolution is not blocked by faith if discussion of it remains in the context of the naturalistic method and its possibilities," Pope John Paul II told the group assembled in Rome for a dialogue on the origins of mankind. He urged the group to continue to study evolution, which he called "serious and urgent". Vatican authorities noted later that the Pope's remarks echoed the teaching of Pope Pius XII, whose 1950 encyclical *Humani Generis* encouraged the study of evolution and said Catholic teaching maintains only that the human soul is created instantaneously by God. They added that Catholic teaching since the 1940's has stressed that the Bible is a religious and moral book, not natural history.

The tragedy is the unwillingness of the qualified experts to brand the creationists as incompetents. Not only have scientists failed us but also those interested in biblical scholarship including the hierarchy of the mainstream churches. Unfortunately these churches, although accepting evolution, remain on the sidelines and avoid an upfront stand. Thus far, only the Episcopal Church has openly supported evolution and condemned creationism. Although the Catholic Church nominally supports evolution, it remains offstage standing in the wings. Two statements by Catholic theologians follow:

"The teaching of evolution is in no way contrary to the Catholic faith. The biblical presentation in Genesis of the creation of the world is not intended, and never was, as a scientific explanation of how the world and all the vegetative, animal, and human life came to be. I think it is recognized that the scientific knowledge in the Bible is primitive. We do not believe the creation stories in the Book of Genesis to be scientific accounts of the principle creation, nor do we think they were intended by the sacred author as such. For reasons, both theological and philosophical, the teaching of evolution in our public schools, does not have anti-religious implications for Catholic students. I think the Church would agree that the teaching of evolution has no inherent anti-religious implications. I firmly believe that sciences and scientific theories presented in public schools, ought to be determined by the scientific and educational community, and not by legislators on the state or federal level." --- Most Reverend Thomas J. O'Brien, Bishop of Phoenix, 1982

"Genesis is not a scientific treatment of the origin or age of the earth, of life, or of mankind. These are the proper subjects for geological and other scientific research, and from such studies valid data and theories may be derived. Creationism does a disservice to religion and theology by interpreting the Bible literally as a 'scientific treatise' rather than strictly as a theological document of Judeo-Christian religious history." --- Father James Skehan, S.J., Boston College

Religionists have the will to believe while scientists have the desire to find out.

If men were immortal, they never would have come into the world.---Galileo, 1632.

If religious people are so happy, why do they pray so much?

Money answers all things. The very moment you believe and send in your love gift, your blessings will begin.---The Right Reverend, Father-in-God, His Divine Eminence, Dr. Frederick J. Eikerenkoetter III of Harlem, a.k.a. Reverend Ike.

Hell is an outrage against humanity...Every step which intelligence has made in Europe from the edge of darkness has been in spite of the church.---Victor Hugo (1802-1885)

Religions die when they are proved to be true. Science is the record of dead religions.---Oscar Wilde (1856-1900)

2

EVOLUTION AND THE LIFE SCIENCES

The universe is a vast and ancient place. We know little of its ultimate origins, but we can clearly state that our species, *Homo sapiens,* has not always been here. We have developed from the grand and magnificent process of evolution which, through the DNA molecule, unites us in a most remarkable way with every other living thing. We are one with all the universe, or if you prefer, with all creation. The evolution of plants and animals is based on a *factual* set of observations. We have an enormous number of facts (for example, millions of fossils) from which to draw, and these fossils paint an enormous, elaborate and consistent picture of change in the orderly succession of all living things up to the present.

In accordance with the equal time law, Reverend Nguba will tell us about special creation according to the Iturabi tribe.

Evolution, as an historical phenomenon, rests upon sound and extensive factual basis as any scientific generalization we know. But our ways of classification of life do not provide for intermediate forms, for example, all animals with feathers are by definition birds. The mechanism of evolution may not be entirely understood but this does not establish special creation. Our notions on the biology of reproduction may be flawed, but this does not prove that babies were brought by the stork. They may have been delivered in a doctor's black bag, discovered amongst the bullrushes or found under cabbage leaves. The *fact* of evolution is well attested by the fossil record and the *theory* of evolution has also been beautifully sustained and expanded over the past century. Geneticists even understand the mechanism in some detail as the genetic code is imprinted in the DNA molecule.

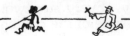

Regarding Miracles: *Fortis imaginatio generat casum,* (A strong imagination begets the event.)---Michel de Montaigne, 1579.

Age of the earth discussion group

Evolution is not only inferred, it has been observed. Witness the fantastic variety of dogs derived from a Siberian wolf-like ancestor. Hundreds of entirely *new* species from tulips to domestic corn have appeared within the span of human history. Corn (*Zya mais*) is one of the most important crops in the world because of its large sweet seeds but these seeds cannot detach themselves from the cobs naturally without human intervention. Without man, this species would be extinct in one year.

Creationists claim that there are no good mutations and, therefore, they do not foster evolution. Most mutations are indeed harmful, but not all. It is estimated that some eight million mutations occur in the human population in each generation. Examples of advantageous mutations are those which have given insects resistance to D.D.T. and have permitted certain plants to grow in heavily poisoned soils near mines.

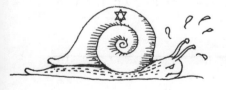

Albert Einstein said: *"A jew is like a snail in a shell. The snail is his race; the shell is his religion."* Unfortunately, Einstein didn't say that it's hell when you get your shell on backwards.

Someone has said that there are three "infinities" — the infinitely large extent of the universe, the infinitely small size of sub-atomic particles, and infinitely complex make-up of living things. The genetic code consists of four amino acids (nitgrogenous bases): adenine, cytosine, guanine and thymine which are the cross-bars in the DNA double helix chain molecule. Hence the code is often said to consist of four "letters" — A, C, G and T which combine to form "words". Even a simple form of life, such as a virus is made up of these letters but the entire word would take a thousand-page volume to write it down. The genetic word within for DNA encoding of the human being is fantastically long. To write it down would require 700 books, each one a thousand pages long.

Evolution does not require elegance, but only that a process works even if poor and illogically. A basic principle of evolution is that, if a structure works at all for a particular function, use it. Then, if possible, improve upon it. Thus we have the pandas thumb which is a sixth digit derived from a wrist bone and adapted through evolution to stripping bamboo leaves which are their only diet.

Evolution is a random walk through time with no ultimate goal in mind. Opportunism is the password — if a living structure works, build on it by natural selection. Legacy of the past precludes optimum design. An interesting aspect of living forms is that the wheel was never invented by evolution as there was no appropriate earlier life structure on which to build. It is virtually impossible to envision modern technology without the wheel. A clock is a microcosm of wheels within wheels. It is possible however, to invent a timepiece with no wheels or moving parts as the modern liquid crystal quartz watches demonstrate. Similarly, animals and plants have evolved internal clocks although we do not fully understand them.

Life has evolved with increasing complexity over the aeons, from simple to more complex forms. In terms of the time-sequence shown in this table, every fossil ever collected is a transitional form — for none has ever violated the sequence. For example, a reptilian fossil has never been found which is older than the oldest amphibian fossil.

FIRST APPEARANCE OF ORGANISMS

	x 1,000,000 years
Microbial (procaryotic cells)	2,700
Complex (eucaryotic cells)	1,400
First multicellular animals	670
Shell-bearing animals	540
Vertebrates (simple fishes)	490
Amphibians	350
Reptiles	310
Mammals	200
Nonhuman primates	60
Earliest apes	25
Australopithcine ancestors	5
Homo sapiens sapiens (modern humans)	0.05 (50,000 years)

(from Creation: Evolution: A View From the National Academy of Science)

Bible: Anti-Feminist
God: "Now therefore kill every male among the little ones, and kill every women that hath known man by lying with him. But all the women children, that have not known man by lying with him, keep for yourselves."---Numbers 31:17-18

There is nothing permanent except change. ---Heraclitus, 540-475 B.C.

Creationists fault evolutionists for not definitely explaining the origin of life even though scientists have had only about two decades to address this problem. This is hardly a valid criticism since evolution is not really concerned with the origin of life, but simply posits the presence of the first simple cell and evolves more complex life therefrom. The creationists argue that the jump from simple organic compounds to the first life, i.e., a repliciting entity like a strand of RNA, is an enormous jump, and indeed it is. They further claim that this leap is so great that the chance of it ever happening is essentially nil. Their answer is, of course, that God created life and God himself, ex-nihilo -- out of nothing. But God is certainly a much greater invention than the first living cell or even man himself. Think of the giant step which would have been involved in generating God out of nothing.

Of all the grand concepts about the nature of the world around us, evolution is the most important, as it determines how we look at ourselves. Back to a flat earth? One could live with that. But life without Darwin? No way! Evolution is a grand theory or paradigm, as is the spherical and heliocentric earth which floats in space and weighs nothing at all. Its surface is without end and yet is finite. The alternative to thinking of life sciences in terms of evolution is not to think at all. This would seem to be the predilection of the fundamentalists -- to believe without thinking.

Creationists make a big deal about the gaps in the fossil record. They accept evolution, as they must for the simple reason of sanity, but they limit it to microevolution, (the appearance of new species but not of new genera, families, orders, or classes) and they speak of macro-gaps. In fact, the reverse is true. Life has undergone macro-evolution and the gaps in the fossil record are only micro-gaps. In a real sense every new fossil dug up supports evolution. Creationism predicts that the total number of species, (some two million today) should decrease over geologic time, as God's creation event recorded in Genesis was a unique one-time affair. Many animals have become extinct over the aeons and a Noachian Flood would add on a catastrophic demise. But the reverse is true! The fossil record shows a general progressive increase in the number of species and their diversity with time. To be sure, some catastrophic killings are in the geologic record, as at the Cretaceous/Tertiary boundary 66.2 million years ago. At that moment in history about one-half of all species were wiped out, presumably by an asteroid striking the earth, but new forms quickly evolved and refilled the vacant ecological niches.

Most significant of all, the book of the rocks reveals the increasing compexity of life over earth history. Fossils of even the simplest forms of life are absent from the earliest rocks. In succession during the Precambian, the first cells appear, then photosynthetic organisms, then cells with nuclei (capable of sexual reproduction), and finally metazoans (animals with more than one cell). During the later periods (Cambrian to the Recent) life slowly evolved in complexity from jellyfish to man.

In summary, evolution and not special creation is compellingly supported by the pyramidal hierarchy of life, increasing speciation with time and life's increasing complexity.

No laws were ever passed saying that evolution had to be taught in biology classes. The prestige of evolutionary theory has been built by its impact on thousands of biologists who have learned its power and usefulness in the study of living things. No laws need to be passed for creationists to do the same thing.---Richard D. Alexander

Science can only ascertain what *is*, but not what should be, and value judgements of all kinds remain outside of its domain.---Albert Einstein, 1950.

What ever knowledge is attainable must be attainable by scientific methods; and what science cannot discover, mankind cannot know.---Bertrand Russell, 1935.

When Pope John Paul II recovered from an assassin's bullet, he ascribed it to the intercession of Mary. But why did Mary let him get shot in the first place?

CREATION AND EVOLUTION

Biblical creation versus evolution -- this has been an acrimonious issue for more than a century between religious fundamentalists who regard the Bible, and especially Genesis, as inerrant and infallible, and the opposed liberal theologians and scientists who regard the Bible as allegorical and symbolic.

The U.S.A. is now dotted with numerous creation institutions, colleges, societies and clubs which demand of their faculties or members the acceptance of the anti-evolution Genesis account of Creation, the Noachian Flood, catastrophic geology, and a very young earth/universe.

Creationists reject that man is related to apes, other mammals, and all forms of life. Preferring to believe that man only was created in the image of God, they abhor the thought of an evolutionary relation to "lower" life. Scientists are well aware of the uniqueness of man, but careful study has shown that our species is built of much the same parts as other animals but modified for a special mode of living. It is the sum of the parts, rather than the components, that distinguishes man from other mammals.

Creationists believe that if the Bible is not accepted as literal truth, then its moral and ethical teachings are also invalid. Liberal and educated Christians, Jews, and Muslims, on the other hand, have no difficulty regarding the Bible as allegorical and symbolic, and yet they derive from it great spiritual and moral lessons.

God has confided in me the ultimate Truth, but I promised not to tell.

During times of stress such as the present many people turn to religion, even pseudoreligion, for comfort. The past two decades saw an astonishing multiplication of new cults and a significant growth of fundamentalism in America. Orthodox religious people usually accept instructions from their leaders who thereby derive prestige and authority as God's spokesmen, but history shows that these leaders are not uniformly wise in their use of this power. One has only to recall American Puritans and the Spanish Inquisition. Creationism has not been revised or altered since the Book of Genesis was composed by primitive tribesman nearly 3,000 years ago. It served well for them because they had no scientific knowledge about natural causes, but it does not serve today as a reliable guide to the history or the nature of the universe.

Science cannot, and does not, pretend that it will be able to answer all of the questions of life. But science is based on skepticism and irreverence for authority and tradition. It rejects the certainty of fundamentalism. Creationism cannot be defined as science because it is based on inflexible presuppositions. The conclusion, derived from biblical inerrancy precedes the search for evidence. When science has split the atom, cracked the genetic code, and put men on the moon, the efforts by creationists to turn back the clock have a certain eerie quality.

(Adapted from Norman Newell, *Creation and Evolution*).

Evolution is the most firmly established truth in the natural universe...---Henry Fairfield Osborn, American paleontologist (1857-1935)

What is it that Jerry Falwell and his ilk among the media evangelists find in the life of Jesus that inspires them to take on the trappings of royalty and the lifestyle of movie stars and millionaires?

4

EVOLUTION HUSHED UP

Sixty years ago, a young biology instructor in Dayton, Tenn., went on trial for the "crime" of teaching evolution to his high school students.

The famous "monkey trial" pitted defense attorney Clarence Darrow against prosecutor William Jennings Bryan and was covered by major journalists including H.L. Mencken. It attracted national -- and even international -- attention.

Although the jury found Scopes guilty, the verdict of history vindicated him and made a laughingstock of the state law that Scopes defied.

Today, most Americans think they can rest assured that their children do have the opportunity to study a subject which is at the cornerstone of modern science.

However, six decades later, the teaching of evolution is still on trial. A study of high school biology textboods reveals this.

The foes of evolution have an enormous influence on what our children read and study in school: Half the biology texts don't cover evolution adequately, and one-sixth don't mention evolution at all.

During 1985, there were attacks on teaching evolution in seven states. Bills restricting the teaching of evolution were introduced in Idaho, Mississippi, and West Virginia, and attorneys for the state of Louisiana appealed a federal district court decision that found that state "creation science" law unconstitutional On the local level, teaching evolution came under attack in school systems including Columbus, Ohio; Cob County, Ga.; and Prescott, Ariz.

This assault on biology textbooks and curricula is the doing of ultrafundamentalists, who either pressure publishers and educators to prevent the teaching of evolution, or demand equal time to be given to "creationsism," which, in its most extreme form, holds that the world and all living things were created in seven days, 10,000 years ago.

Evolution is an essential part of the science of biology, helping to explain why certain traits are passed along from generation to generation, how species develop new characteristics in response to a changing environment, and, ultimately, how new species emerge from existing forms of life.

Trying to teach biology without evolution is like teaching physics without using the law of gravity. Giving "equal time" to creationism is like teaching the flat-earth theory in a geography class -- or giving astrology equal time with astronomy.

Unfortunately, the censorship of evolution is only one symptom of the decline of science textbooks. Instead of intellectually stimulating classroom materials that encourage students to learn for themselves about the wonders of the natural world, science texts have degenerated into pedagogical pabulum that encourages memorization and rote learning.

In addition to downplaying evolution, today's biology texts -- and a growing number of

Searching for God in this universe is like a blind man in a dark room looking for a black cat that isn't there.

texts in chemistry, physics and other sciences -- fail to explain what a theory is, what an experiment is, and why science is, above all, a method of testing out explanations of how the world works.

Not surprisingly, the deterioration of science textbooks has coincided with a de-emphasis upon lab work -- an essential part of any science education worthy of the name.

This dismal trend is a reversal of the renaissance in science education that began during the late 1950s and was prompted by concern over the Soviet challenge to America's technological supremacy.

Now, more than ever before, America's young people need excellence in science education to prepare them for the high-technology jobs of the future. Young Americans cannot prepare to meet the challenges of the 21st century by studying science textbooks that offer less coverage of evolution than John Scopes tried to provide his students six decades ago.

Wayne Moyer
(reprinted by permission)

BEATITUDES

I. Blessed are those who place faith above reason for they shall be called Christians.

II. Blessed are the naive for they shall believe in miracles.

III. Blessed are the sanctimonious for they shall spout stained-glass blather.

IV. Blessed are those who go around in circles for they shall be known as wheels.

V. Blessed are those who believe in the unbelievable, for they shall have a free lunch.

Prisoner of Blasphemy:
In 1842 George Holyoake was convicted by a jury of blasphemy, the last such conviction in Great Britain. The words he uttered were: "I am of no religion and I do not believe there is such a thing as a God. If I had my way, I would place the Diety on half-pay, as the government of this country did with the subaltern officers." Holyoake served six months in prison in Gloucester, England.

"You ask whether I shall discuss 'man'," Darwin wrote to Alfred Russel Wallace late in 1857. "I think I shall avoid the whole subject, as it is so surrounded with prejudices; though I fully admit that it is the highest and most interesting problem for the naturalist." True to his resolve, Darwin said nothing about man in the *Origin of Species* (1859) except to note that: "Light will be thrown on the origin of man and his history."

Congress shall make no law respecting the establishment of a religion...No religious test shall ever be required as a qualification for any office of public trust under the United States.---U.S. Constitution

---

Luckily, the majority of nominal Christians has at no time taken the Christian ideology seriously. Religion, it seems to me, can only survive as a consciously accepted system of make believe.---Aldous Huxley

5

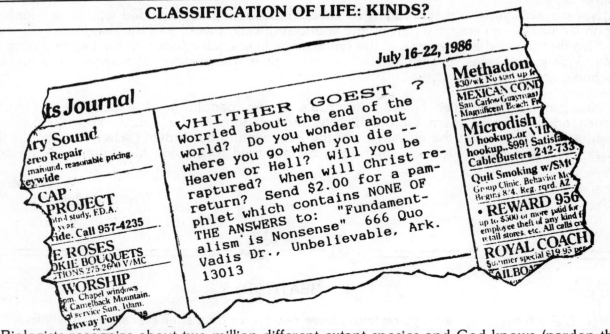

Biologists recognize about two million different extant species and God knows (pardon the expression) how many extinct forms. Paleontologists estimate that only 1 percent al all animals which have existed on earth are now living. There are 9,000 living species of birds but an estimated 1.2 million species probably have existed since their first appearance in the Jurassic, 150 million years ago. Creationists do not accept the usual scientific classification of life into kingdoms, phyla, classes, orders, families, genera, and species. Instead they speak only of "kinds" as this is the biblical term -- hence, we have the dog-kind, the cat-kind, etc. God must have loved the beetle-kind as there are 500,000 species.

Creationists avoid using the standard Linnean latinized scientific nomenclature for animals but talk only of the biblical kinds. Apparently "kinds" sometimes means species, sometimes genus, sometimes even family or order but it is never clear, as their definitions are vague. The creationists have never yet produced an explicit biological definition of a kind. Now, if they don't know what a kind is, how can they recognize one, let alone claim that there is biological evidence that kinds cannot be changed by evolutionary processes.

Scientists recognize the existence of about two million different species of plants and animals, while creationists accept perhaps a few hundred different "kinds". A testimony at the Arkansas creation-evolution trial in 1981 seems pertinent:

Annis, (an attorney for the plaintiff): "Some creationists believe that "kinds" are synonomous with species or genera and some with family and some with order, don't they?"

Fryar (creationist(: "Among the scientists with whom I am working...well... it tends more toward the family, but it may go to order in some cases."

Annis: "You've been studying turtles for many years, haven't you?"

Fryar: "Yes".

Annis:"Is the turtle an originally created kind?"

Fryar: "I'm working on that."

Annis: "Are all turtles within the same created kind?"

Fryar: "That is what I am working on."

Like other creationist scientists cross-examined, Fryar was unable to define "kind" or explain how his research will ever lead to an explanation of this fuzzy concept. Scientists classify bats as a flying mammal within the order Chiroptera of which there are nearly one thousand species. The creationists apparently recognize but one kind...the bat kind. Until "kind" can be defined in an operationally testable manner, no reserach can be conducted either to verify or falsify the creationists claims.

Duane Gish, of the Institute for Creation Research, gives examples of "kinds" as variously being species, genera, families, and classes. He then concludes that, "We cannot always be sure what constitutes a separate kind." It appears that when creationists argue that variation in living organisms is limited to "kinds", their logic is circular. If creationists wish to perform a real service to science, let them put away their debate teams and batteries of attorneys and get down to research. A good first project would be to definitively classify life according to "kinds".

Perhaps the most convincing evidence for evolution is that all life can be so readily classified. Creationists reject this hierarchical and vertical classification, but simply would classify them horizontally into the biblical "kinds". This, of course, is tantamount to no classification at all. To them, life is a one-story building but to biologists it is a high-rise. No reasonable person questions man as being a humanoid, a primate, a mammal and an animal.

We read in Genesis (2:19) that God commanded Adam to name all of the animals, "each according to its kind". Whatsoever Adam called every living creation, "that was the name thereof." One can only speculate on how Adam named the bat. Did its blindness move him to call it *murcielago* (Sp.); its baldness *chauve-souris* (Fr.); its shyness *pipistrelloe* (It.); its leathery skin *Laderlapp* (Swed.); its preference for the night *nukteris* (Gr.); its resemblance to the mouse *Fladermaus* (Ger.); the sound of its flapping wings *watwat* (Arab.); its winglike hands *chiroptera* (Gr. *chir*, hand, plus *pteron*, wing)? Adam must have been reincarnated frequently to come up with all these names.

Creationists classify the bat as only the bat kind. Scientists recognize bats as mammals in the order *Chiroptera* which can be further subdivided into families, genera and species. The species of bats number about 1000, making them speciation-wise the second most successful of all the twenty orders of extant mammals --- after the rodents with about 2000 species.

Creationists accept evolution (so-called micro-evolution) within any particular kind and it is only macro-evolution that they object to. So the 1000 types of bats up to the order level have evolved! This is tantamount to accepting complete Darwinian evolution.

So long as Jesus had to die for our sins, it is probably a good thing that he died on the cross rather than by stoning. Otherwise Catholics, rather than crossing themselves, would have to go around hitting their heads with rocks. ---Father J. Fulton O'Hara

One of the most arrogant and false assumptions is the contention that religion and ethics are inseparable and that only the pious are virtuous. Fundamentalists assume that religious instruction makes men morally good. But our prisons are crowded with devout inmates while the non-theist is a rare jail bird.

Predictions in the Bible are on a par with those in fortune cookies. They lend themselves to all sorts of circumstances.

MICRO/MACRO EVOLUTION

Creationists accept what they choose to call micro-evolution but disbelieve macro-evolution--terms not clearly defined. But micro-evolution apparently means horizontal evolution whereby there is variation within species but without generation of any new species. Of course they would be laughed off the debate platform if they did not accept such micro-evolution. All one needs to do is observe the varieties within the human race, between two brothers or sisters or to observe the varieties of dogs, cats, horses, etc. It is obvious that life is plastic and highly changeable. But there has also been major historical evolution not only to create new species, but genera as well. For example, the common corn or maize *(Zya mais)* has evolved in the past thousand years. The ancestral plant from which corn was derived remains uncertain but it probably was the grass, *teosinte* of Mexico. Corn can no longer seed itself and, if it were not for the hands of man it would become extinct in one year. Corn is the world's fourth most important basic starch crop, after rice, wheat, and potatoes.

By genetic manipulation (polyploidy) entirely new plants have been generated. Cabbages *Brassica oryecea)* have been successfully crossed with turnips *(Brassica rapa)* to create the swede or rutabaga *(Brassica napus)* -- a vegetable common in England. Many other examples could be cited.

If only micro-evolution has occured the realm of life would be a horizontal structure like a Levittown suburbia. But, instead, life on earth is a pyramid -- a hierarchy ascending from individual to species to genera to family to order to class to phylum and to kingdom. Ronald Reagan, for example, is of the caucasion race, of the *sapiens* species, of the *Homo* genus, of the humanoid family, of the primate order, of the mammalian class, of the vertebrate phylum and of the animal kingdom. The fact that we can readily classify all life forms known, or presumably yet undiscovered, into an existing hierarchal pyramid is compelling evidence for macro-evolution.

Life is exceedingly plastic and gradational as one would expect of evolving forms. In a famous experiment the Russian biologist Karpenchenko produced a plant (a tetraploid hybrid) which had a radish top and a cabbage root. This cross was given a new genus name *Raphanobrassica,* which means radish-cabbage. When creationists admitted to micro-evolution, they forfeited their cause. Macro-evolution is simply micro-evolution over a longer time span.

PURPOSE OF SEX

The opinion of the Pope not withstanding, the purpose of sex is *not* reproduction (which can be achieved in nature asexualy) but to re-shuffle the genes and provide new genetic combinations in the resulting offspring. Sexual recombination, of course, fuels evolution, permitting it to occur one thousand times faster than with asexually reproducing organisms.

Death from old age never befalls asexual forms such as bacteria, blue-green algae or, usually, amoebas. They multiply simply by dividing equally and passing their substance on to daughter cells. Such life forms may be killed by a hostile environment but they never die of old age. They are truly immortal.

Asexual reproduction by simple cell division produces a clone. Artificial cloning has been successfully achieved by biologists even in mammals — e.g. rabbits. Such virgin birth is conceivable (no pun intended) even for man, as virtually every cell in our body contains the genetic code. But all such virgin births would be no more than the genetic mimic of the parent.

Death of individuals is good for the species and the ability to evolve is essential for species to adapt to changing environmental conditions and to produce ever more complex forms. The death of individuals is necessary for the survival of life itself. Concepts of heaven, hell, and life after death, no matter how appealing to the human psyche, are totally without merit in the Darwinian scheme of life. Only our genes are immortal, passed along from generation to generations of life, back to 3.5 billion years ago.

It shall be unlawful for any teacher in...public schools in the state,...to teach the theory [of evolution] that denies the story of the devine creation of man as taught in the Bible, and to teach instead that man has descended from a lower order of animals.---Act of the Legislature of Tennessee, 1925.---Scopes' Monkey Trial.

8

CHICKEN OR EGG FIRST?

A classical debate asks, Which came first, the chicken or the egg? In terms of evolution, the answer is perfectly clear. The egg came first because it is within the egg that the genetic variations occur, or as biologists say, the chicken is the egg's strategy for begatting another egg. If a chicken reproduced simply by cloning itself all offspring would be precise carbon-copies of their parents and there would be little evolutionary change.

To believe that acquired characteristics can be inherited is called Lamarckism which is in contrast to Darwinism. The giraffe does not have a long neck because living giraffes stretch their necks ever higher for browsing off the leaves of trees; rather giraffes which genetically inherited longer necks succeeded better in the marketplace of natural selection. Similarly a child would not be any stronger if his father does 100 push-ups each day, because acquired strength is not inherited. All birds, including chickens, were derived from reptiles. This did not happen of course in one large jump, but by miniscule changes over millions of generations. These changes were gradual but somewhere along the line, for purposes of classification, a bird-like reptile became a reptile-like bird.

The old adage, "scarce as hens teeth," is an oblique way of saying that something is non-existent. All modern birds have thorny beaks totally devoid of teeth. But recently it was discovered that chickens possess a full set of genes to produce teeth. By laboratory manipulation, these genes can be "turned-on" to produce peg-like reptilian teeth in the mouth tissue of the chicken. Apparently, in the course of evolution, birds became toothless, not because they lost genes responsible for producing teeth, but by losing the regulator genes that controlled the time and place of tooth production during embryological development. Why would a Creator, during the special creation of modern birds, endow them with a highly complex piece of genetic machinery that would never be used?

A similar situation pertains to whales and dolphins. Their front legs are modified into flippers but all that is left of their hind legs are minute traces of the pelvic girdle and the thigh bones buried deep in the animal's body. Yet, about 1 to 400 whales and dolphins develop hind legs. Usually these are small structures still completely buried in the body. If the Creator specifically created great whales, why did he give them the genetic mechanism to produce hind legs? They obviously have no use for these appendages and in fact, they are a hinderance. Like the tooth genes of birds, these represent genetic baggage left over from remote ancestors.

By the use of fossils, paleontologists have traced the origin of whales to camel-like ungulates of the early Cenozoic Era. Creationists find this hilarious, but consider the hippopotamus. This is an animal which lives by day in water and forages on dry land at night. Their nostrils have migrated to the top of their head so that they can breathe almost fully submerged. The hippoes even give birth to their young beneath water. Here is a land animal that is already half adapted to life in the water.

In Genesis 1:20 God created birds, so He obviously created the hen first, capable of laying and hatching her own eggs. Thus life began with adult full-grown fruit trees, adult animals and Adam and Eve. This order of events stands in contrast to the evolution scenario.

*Thank **me**, it's Friday.*

EVOLUTION: BICYCLE TO AIRPLANE

Dean Fraser (University of Indiana) has written that the airplane is an evolutionary development that began with the bicycle. The Wright Brothers were bicycle mechanics and their first aircraft was essentially a flying bicycle. In the early years, the airplane was hardly more than a curiosity and the number of these frail machines in existence was miniscule until World War I. They were constructed of wood and cloth and so were ill-adapted to be preserved against the ravages of time and neglect.

Only with the development of all metal planes in the 1930s was it conceivable that a wrecked airplane would be preserved indefinitely, buried beneath sediments. Future generations of archeologists in their diggings might well discover the remains of a World War II B-17 or a Boeing 747 jet plane. Their chances of finding the original aircraft flown by the Wright Brothers in 1903 in Kitty Hawk, North Carolina is nil. Were it not for the history and the photographic record, the "fossil evidence" would lead us to the conclusion that the aircraft appeared suddenly by special creation as an elaborate and perfected form having no linkage with any possible forebearer such as the bicycle.

Sketch of the Smithsonian mechanical Pteradactyl. Wingspan 18 feet, weight 44 lbs.

Evolution aside for a moment, another metal bird of a different feather is the half-size replica of a 100 million year old pteradactyl made for the Smithsonian Institution that could actually fly. Unfortunately it soon crashed and was destroyed proving that Mesozoic reptiles can be "born again" and become extinct twice.

Son William, if you and your friends are faithful to me you will make an end of priests and priestcraft to the end of the world.---Sir William Penn (1621-1670) Father of the founder of Pennsylvania.

The religions of the world have 27 holy books which they consider the word of God or gods. Christians accept only one as authentic, the Bible. Atheists reject all 27, so Christians and atheists share a broad area of agreement. Statistically speaking, their views are less than 4 percent apart.

He was of the faith chiefly in the sense that the church he currently did not attend was Catholic. ---Kingsley Amis

The nearer a nation is to Rome the more impious are the people.---Machiavelli (1469-1527)

Erasmus Darwin, the grandfather of Charles, was a noted scientist with inklings of evolution. He authored the classic work *Zoonomia* which was acclaimed by being translated into German, French and Italian. The Pope "honored" this landmark scientific treatise by placing it on the *Index Expurgatorius*.

10

GAPS IN THE FOSSIL RECORD: GISH'S LAW

Great progress has been made by the paleontologists in filling gaps in the fossil record. Nonetheless, creationists lean heavily upon "missing links" and claim that no species was ever derived from another. They assert that there has only been a decrease by extinction in the total number of species. The rarity of intermediate forms has an obvious scientific explanation. The acquisition of new successful genetic links is rare, so that any population of individuals with adaptions would typically be small and restricted to a highly localized area. Only when an accumulation of advantageous traits results in real survival value do the mutants begin to radiate, compete successfully and increase in numbers exponentially. Few missing links have properties and locations favorable for fossilization.

Duane T. Gish, author of *Evolution: The Fossils Say No!*, is a leading proponent of so-called scientific creationism. In his debates he invariably uses a hilarious cartoon lampooning evolution and entitled "From Fish to Gish" which brings down the house and scores a few points. His chief thrust, however, is to attempt to lose evolution down a gap in the fossil record. Creationists refer to their own concept of origins by special creation as a model. They apparently prefer this to the term "theory" because a model requires no evidence, and need not even by workable. A model airplane need not to be able to fly.

Of late, paleontologists have enjoyed good success in closing some of the gaps in the fossil record. Witness the discovery of Triassic protomammals in the Kayenta Formation of Arizona and of early marsupials on an island between South America and Antartica. These finds were not serendipitous as their probable presence was predicted before the digging commenced. This sounds like the Right Stuff.

Gish, however, would see it differently — there are now more gaps than ever before. His reasoning is that if fossils A and C exist there is only one gap. But if B is discovered then there are 2 gaps — between A and B and between B and C.

We can apply this reasoning nicely to the Class Aves. Some 9,000 species of birds are now extant and it is estimated that 1.2 million species (more than 99 percent extinct) have existed since the likes of *Archaeopteryx* in the Jurassic. If all 1,200,000 species are ever found by paleontologists we will end up with 1,199,999 gaps. There is something about this which saddens.

In deference to Duane T. Gish, we can offer Gish's law: "As the fossil record becomes ever more complete, the number of gaps increases."

I'm not anti-semitic! Some of my best friends are Palestinians.

11

BALANCED TREATMENT

The proposal for balanced treatment of evolution and creationism in schools, which temporarily became law in both Arkansas and Louisiana, was based on model legislation prepared by creationist Ellwanger of North Carolina. He also prepared model legislation which, if ever passed, would require that any federal monies appropriated to support museums and scientific research must be matched by federal funding for creation displays and research. This, for example, would mean that the Smithsonian Institution in Washington would have to establish a "Great Hall for Special Creation" -- presumably the biblical version. And the National Science Foundation would have to find creation research projects that conceivably could be supported. This must remain speculative as no one has ever submitted a grant proposal on creationism to the National Science Foundation, but it might:

1. Establish a Christian theme park ("Six Flags Over Jesus") next to Oral ("Expect-a-miracle") Roberts University outside of Tulsa, Oklahoma. The central motif could be a 700-foot high Jesus, an exact replica of the apparition experienced by Roberts. Package a miracle with each box of Cracker Jacks.

2. Retain Peter Ueberroth to plan a gala celebration in 1996 to celebrate the 6,000-year anniversary of the creation of the earth and universe. The ceremony and TV special should climax at 0900 hours, October 23, the actual hour and calendar date of Creation in 4,004 B.C. Most appropriately, the celebration would be staged in California -- the Granola State (Fruit, Nuts and Flakes).

3. Place a crucifix on the top of the Washington Monument and add the head of Jesus the presidential sculptures at Mount Rushmore.

4. Establish a permanent art exhibit at Tabernacle Square in Salt Lake City of Mormon religious pioneer paintings and Soviet women-drivers-tractor realism. Here the pious could compare the two genres to learn the differences, if any.

5. Establish 37 more national religious holidays.

"Okay, you guys, get over here if you want to get in the picture."

6. Hold an annual walk-on-water contest for superstars of the electronic church. The penance for those who fall through would be that they must actually sign all those letters they write soliciting funds. Disqualify any contestants who know where the rocks are.

7. Re-name all Mexican women Maria who are not already so-named.

8. Build a full-scale replica of Noah's Ark out of camphor wood and caulked with pitch. House all of the two million kinds of animals for one year while afloat on Lake Michigan.

9. Set up a study group of born-again Christians to oversee the excavations at Dinosaur National Monument in Utah and keep the paleontologists from hiding any human tracks and bones dug up. This group would also expose any cheating done in the reconstructions and, most importantly, learn how the paleontologists discover dinosaur names.

10. Make a study to determine if the Bhagwan Shri Rajneesh's 92 Rolls Royces are really enough, in deference to his exhalted mission here on earth. Bear in mind, too, that while Jesus saves and Moses invests, the Bhagwan spends and the Mongol hordes.

11. Funnel adequate funds to the Institute of Creation Research to send further expeditions to Mt. Ararat to search for Noah's Ark and to the jungles of the Congo to capture living dinosaurs.

12. Establish a research chair at Bob Jones University to determine how many angels can dance on the head of a pin.

13. Build the world's most powerful microscope to reveal the inner realm of the DNA double helix; for certainly within this giant molecule hides man's soul.

14. Comandeer the Palomar 200-inch telescope to search for Heaven, the Celestial Spheres and the Firmament which separates our realm from the Void.

15. Erect a Chapel in Sedona, Arizona, built entirely from surplus "pieces of the true cross" now gathering dust in the reliquaries of European cathedrals.

16. Study the tooth of Buddha from the temple at Kandy in Sri Lanka to see why it looks so much like that of a pig.

17. Hire a bunchful of gnomes to dig a shaft ever deeper beneath Yellowstone National Park down, down, down, to the upper level of Hell.

18. A National Prayers Day could be established. For example, on Christmas Eve, everyone in the U.S. could pray that it would snow on Miami Beach on Christmas at noon. This has never happened historically, so if it did, Doubting Thomases would finally be convinced of the efficacy of prayer.

19. A photographer could be permanently assigned to Oral Roberts to photograph one of the periodic apparitions of Jesus to him. God apparently does not answer letters, but perhaps He would appear for a photographic opportunity or to be recorded on tape.

20. Keepers of religious relics such as pieces of the true cross or the Shroud of Turin could have these tested by carbon-14 to see if they are in fact 2000 years old. With the present-day techniques only a single thread from the shroud would be required. After all, there is no reason to fear reality. Or is there?

21. Determine how many times Jerry Falwell was born and if Moses was an Egyptian.

Presidential Debate, Oct. 1988

Jessie Jackson: I say prayer in schools and bingo every Tuesday morning.
Pat Robertson: I say prayer, Bible study and hymns in school.
Jackson: I say flag, motherhood and the U.S. Marines.
Robertson: I say America, traditional family values and the Fourth of July!
Jackson: And I say God Bless America. Hozanna on High!
Robertson: And I say, Onward Christian Soldiers, Praise the Lord, Jesus is King!

On Faith, Hope and Charity: I have no faith, very little hope, and as much charity as I can afford.---Thomas Huxley (1825-1895)

*Behemoth
or Cockatrice*

Behemoth (Job 40:15-24): Behold now behemoth...he eateth grass as an ox...he moveth his tail like a cedar: the sinews of his stones are wrapped together...his bones are like bars of iron. He is the chief of the ways of God...Behold, he drinketh up the river Jordan and hasteth not.

*Behemoth
Job 40:15-24*

Paper Dragon

13

GLOSSARY

Archbishop: A Christian ecclesiastic of a rank superior to that attained by Christ. --- H.L. Menken

Centaur: An animal of the Bible which is half man and half horse, with human foreparts and a horse-like posterior but now regarded by most authorities as extinct. If extinct, only recently so, because as historical records reveal Hernando Cortez in his conquest of Mexico lead a cavalry with more horses asses than horses.

Church: A place in which Gentlemen who have never been in Heaven brag about it to persons who will never get there. --- H.L. Mencken

Dreamer: An evolutionist who asks for equal time in the pulpit on a Sunday morning.

Eden: A luxuriant garden where the Devil experiments with the seeds of new sins and encourages the growth of stable vices.

Evangelist: A country bumpkin of the wacko-right turned religious huckster and usually named Billy who, draping the mantle of Christian piety around his shoulders and stomping off on a witch hunt, ferrets out secular humanists and other miscellaneous bogeyman. With a primitive view of this world and a psychodelic view of the next, he harangues lost sinners in an impassioned and declamatory style to repent and be born again. Ranting and raving, and spouting smoke and fury, he paces the stage like a whirling dervish run amock. Then he threatens with hell-fire and brimstone. Wow! Jimmy ("send-in-the-buck") Swaggert-a-mania at its best! And after the fat lady sings, they coax him back in his cage. Sigh!

Fundamentalist: A backwoods rustic living among 'possums, 'coons, armadillos and magnolias who is functionally illiterate. A boll-weevil southerner who believes in biblical literalism and is suffused with hatred.

Guru: One who, on looking into a mirror, sees not only his own reflection but a reflection of his reflection reflected in his own eyeglasses.

Haiti: An island country in the Caribbean which remains under the influence of Voodoo Catholicism. It achieved economic and social success by throwing off the yoke of white colonial domination and slavery in the 1820's. It was successively and successfully ruled by Grampa Doc, Papa Doc, and Baby Doc — the rule being one man, one vote, one party. As a major trading partner of the United States, Haiti imports aid and exports AIDS.

Harangue: Florid oratory with more gusto than decorum by a televangelist in which Ultimate Truth is demonstrated by thunderous conviction. In its finest form it is known as an orangutan.

Holy Ghost: His Indescribable Holiness.

Homo sapiens: (1) Man, the wise. (2) Man, the sap.

Lachryma Christi: A Campanian dark golden wine of fruity bouquet with no particular pedigree but with an amusing pretense. "The tears of Christ, my boy, the tears of Christ", said Brother Partridge, savoring a soupçon "'tis a strange name for a wine grown on the slopes of Vesuvius, which is as near to hell as any living soul can get."

Mackerel snapper: A pejorative name applied to members of a certain christian sect (which shall remain unnamed) who formerly were divinely abjured from eating meat on Fridays. But, Oh happy day!, now they can. It was discovered that God was only kidding.

Mesmerism: Hypnotism before he wore good clothes, kept a carriage and asked Incredulity out to dinner. --- A. Bierce

Moral Majority: The John Birch Society wrapped in the flag of the church.

Orangutan: By some authorities regarded as an anthropoid ape *(Pongo pygmaeus)*, but according to the natives of Borneo and Sumatra, the orangutan is actually a human who remains speechless to avoid payment of taxes.

Parthenogenesis: Birth from virgin females without fertilization by a male spermatozoa. It occurs commonly in certain insects, crustaceans, worms, gastropods, and some reptiles. In principle it also could happen in mammals and man. By genetic law, the offspring is *always* female. Jesus, as a male, would be an impossibility.

Preacher: A person who thinks twice before saying nothing.

Sacrilege: A blind from which fundamentalism can shoot arrows at evolutionists accusing them of blasphemy without fear of reprisal by claiming special privilege.

Sunday School: A prison in which children do penance for the evil conscience of their parents. --- H.L. Mencken

Theology: Episcopopagy which begins with assumptions and ends in the fog. Theology is classified superstition which belongs in the dustbin with alchemy and astrology. The art of explaining the Unknowable in terms of things not worth knowing to people with a stupendous capacity for believing the incredible.

Trinity: Father, Son, and Holy Ghost — making in all, one.

Vatican Wine Cellar: A moldy dungeon beneath St. Peters Cathedral where the Grapes of Wrath are stored.

Wheelbarrow: An Egyptian chariot. First practical application of the wheel. Among the greatest of inventions, as it taught the Israelites to walk on their hind legs.

A butcher-bird impaling its victim on a thorn, or a lion killing a gazelle, or a cat biting a mouse, or a tick feeding on the eye of a fowl or an intestinal worm eating in the entrails of a priest are as much a part of the cosmic "order" as stars moving in space, and are a part of the "divine plan" which theists say exists. ---Woosley Teller

The most preposterous notion that *Homo sapiens* has ever dreamed up is that the Lord God of Creation, Shaper and Ruler of all the Universe, wants the saccharine adoration of His creatures, can be swayed by their prayers, and becomes petulant if he does not receive this flattery. Yet this absurd fantasy, without a shred of evidence to bolster it, pays all the expenses of the oldest, largest and least productive industry in all history. ---Lazarus Long

Due to a shortage of devoted "sheep", the production of gurus has been discontinued.

Censorship makes children of us all.

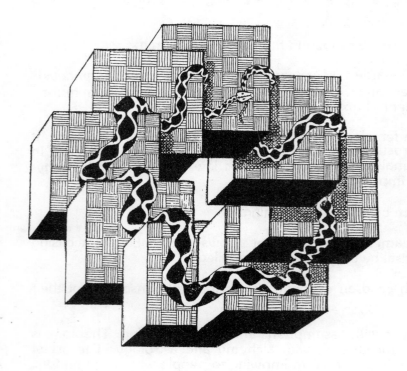

A Lord's Prayer for Schools

Our Father, who art in Heaven,
Hello, what is your name?
By thinking none, we will be dumb
In class, as they are in Heaven.
Give us this day our daily bread $$
And Lord, give us no school buses
As we will give no school buses
To them that have busses against us
Teach us nothing but Special Creation
And deliver us from Evolution
For thine is the Republic,
And the power of Old Glory
Forever and ever. Amen.

Ask Professor Nobel Price:
Q. How do I tell whether I am in a religious or a scientific meeting? *—A Bit Confused*
A. It's easy. In a religious meeting everyone laughs, smiles, and claps on cue. People nod their heads "yes," and shout "Amen!" And it is not over until the fat lady sings.
    In a scientific seminar everyone scowls, shakes his head "no," and say "No way." And when it's over, they all walk over and hit their heads against the wall.

God is love
    In Yellowstone Park, a grizzly bear attacked a child at a campsite and chewed off his leg. His parents watched terrified but hopelessly. They prayed but to no avail. The boy bled to death. God was there. He is omnipresent. God is love.
    At the San Diego Wild Animal Park a little girl watched in fright as a wolf tore a rabbit to shreds in a bloody spectacle. "Why did the wolf kill the bunny" the child asked her mother. "The rabbit must have sinned," she replied. God knew, He is omniscient. He is not dead. He just doesn't want to get involved. God is love.

    When Columbus sailed the ocean blue, priests fell to their knees and prayed that he would not fall over the edge.---Joseph Lewis (1889-1972)

    If a minister believes and teaches evolution, he is a stinking skunk, he is a hypocrite and a liar.---Rev. Billy Sunday, 1925.

    When a certain shameless fellow asked a pious old man what God had done before the creation of the world, the latter aptly countered that He had been building Hell for the curious.---John Calvin, Institutes, I, 1536.

PART 5

PHILOSOPHY OF SCIENCE

1

PHILOSOPHY OF SCIENCE

When a theory is no longer amenable to change or modification by new evidence, it is no longer science. Fallibility is the hallmark of science. Conclusive evidence always eludes us. No theory in the history of science had enjoyed a more spectacular career than Newton's celestial mechanics. But Newton's laws had to give way to Einstein's. During the Dark Ages, it was the bible, not Aristotle, that provided the final word on the past, present and future. To oppose a strict interpretation of the Bible was not only dangerous, it could even be fatal. In 1632, Galileo was forced by the Spanish Inquisition to publicly disavow his belief that the earth revolved around the sun. Today the evangelical creationists are even more insistent upon a strict hyperliteral interpretation of the Bible — much more so than the Catholic Church ever was. The flood of Noah is now to creationists not only an unquestioned truth but, in fact, an obsession. Of late, science has shown that the world is ruled by natural and even by mathematical laws which leave no room for revealed truth. Science does not allow for miracles, rather it seeks to explain miracles in natural terms. Unlike the fundamentalists, the mainstream churches now attempt to build Christianity on an authority resting on scientific fact rather than on supernatural revelations.

Creationists like to pose the question: *Quo vadis?* and then go on to spin yarns about how they think the world should be, or how they would like it to be. Darwinism, to the dismay of many nice but naive people, tells it like it is. It explains why we are born, live and die; why we spend but a moment on the stage of life; why there are two sexes; and why nature has no need for the hypotheses of heaven, hell, and everlasting life. And why nature is "red of tooth and claw" rather than a benign Walt Disney world.

To argue, as creationists do, that a theory must be true owing to authority rather than to compelling evidence is antithetical to science. Unwillingness to revise a theory to accommodate observation is to forfeit any claim to be scientific. Creationists do not participate in scientific enterprise, as they do not publish papers in the refereed scientific journals. The

major annoyance is that they present themselves as "scientific". The evangelist regards evolution as "godless, atheistic and communistic" but the last society to prohibit the teaching of Darwinism was the Soviet Union under the sway of Lysenko during Stalin's regime. The argument was that evolution contradicted communist dogma and the result was a 30 year set-back for Soviet biology and agriculture. Russia still cannot feed herself, but must import food from the West. The object lesson is clear.

Science is no longer the servant of religion, but it still contributes immeasurably to a wise and philosophical perspective of life. Why does nature let us write down her deepest secrets on a single page of paper or by a single equation? Someday the door will surely open and expose a glittering central mechanism of the universe in all its beauty and simplicity.

Scientists are aware of the uniqueness of the human condition, science cannot and does not pretend that it will ever be able to answer all the questions of life. Scientists cannot escape humility and as groping philosophers they accept a limit to understanding. We are thankful for the mysteries that still lie beyond our grasp. Beauty lies in the eyes of the beholder but also it increases with understanding.

Modern man is not the pawn of his environment but rather the author of it. We are no longer subject to survival of the fittest. We can command our future and truly be self-made men. Survival of our species is our common cause. Science is concerned with answering how but not why. It is neither moral nor immoral but amoral. It does not profess to be able to determine goals or purpose in what it discovers. The search is for proximal truth, not ultimate Truth.

Robert Schadewald writes that creation "science" and conventional science differ. Science is wedded, at least in principle, to evidence. Creationism is wedded to doctrine, as evidenced by the statement of belief required for membership by various creationist organizations. Because creationism is first and foremost a matter of biblical faith, evidence from the natural world is only of secondary importance. Authoritarian systems like creationism instill in their adherents a peculiar view of truth. Whatever advances the cause is true; whatever damages the cause is false. From this viewpoint, errors should be covered up when possible and only acknowledged when failure to do so threatens greater damage to the cause. If colleagues spread errors, it is better not to criticize them publicly. Better to have followers deceived than to have them question the legitimacy of their leaders. In science, fame accrues to those who overturn errors. In dogmatic systems, one who unnecessarily exposes an error to the public is a traitor or an apostate. It is significant that, as with the "Nebraska Man" fiasco and the "Piltdown Man" hoax, errors in science are uncovered and corrected from within the scientific community. In contrast, creationists rarely expose their own errors, and they sometimes fail to correct them when others expose them.

QUOTES of ROBERT INGERSOLL (1833-1899)

The star that shines above that dawn, the herald of the day, is Science, not superstition; Reason, not religion.

Theology is, always has been, and always will be ignorant, arrogant, puerile, and cruel. When the church had power, hypocrisy was crowned and honesty imprisoned. Fraud wore the tiara and truth was the convict. Liberty was in chains. Theology has always sent the worst to heaven and the best to hell.

An honest God is the noblest work of man.

The mystery of life and death we cannot comprehend. This chaos called world has never been explained. The golden bridge of life from gloom emerges. Beyond this we do not know. Fate is speechless, destiny is dumb, and the secret of the future has never been told. We love, we wait, we hope. All paths, whether filled with thorns or flowers, end here. The rag of wretchedness and the purple robe of power are differences lost in the democracy of death. Character survives; goodness lives; love is immortal.

A believer is a bird caged. A freethinker is an eagle parting the clouds with a tireless wing.

The Bible cannot be cited as a source for truth until the Bible itself is proven to be true.

Well, I'll give you my opinion sir. Baptism is a good thing, with lots of soap.

Each nation has created a God, and the God has always resembled his creators.

If we were inhabitants of a primitive culture, we probably would believe in a God with three heads, rather than a three-headed God — the Trinity.

The principle business of priests is to boast about their God, and to claim that He could easily vanquish all other Gods.

Priests have invented a crime called "blasphemy" and, within that blind, hypocrisy has crouched for two thousand years.

God so loved the world that he made up his mind to damn most of us.

--- Robert Ingersoll

Why does matter and the material universe, which is known to exist, need a creator? Why can't it always have existed? And why is it that God does not need a creator even though His existence is unknown?

Ask Prof. Nobel Price:
   Q. What is the difference between the Apostle Paul and Rev. Norman Vincent Peale?
   A. Paul was appealing; Peale was appaling.
   Q. What was the cause of Pat Robertson's accident recently?
   A. He was hit by a motorboat while walking his duck.

117

AGE OF REASON

Religion began 50,000 years ago with Neanderthal man, the first pre-historic man to bury his dead. Man is the only animal who realizes that one day he is going to die. Religion had its origin in mythology, mysticism and fear — especially the fear of death. We now live in a post-religious era, an Age of Reason with man relying upon the data of science.

Science offers evidence without certainty; religion offers certainty without evidence. As a fluid search for the truth, science remains tentative — there are no absolute facts. We thought we understood gravity but Einstein's geometric (fictitious force) concept of gravity has replaced Newton's (real force) concept. But is this the final answer? Almost certainly not. There are more grand theories or paradigms to come but these will be discovered through scientific inquiry and not by omphaloskepsis or thaumaturgy. Such new central-organizing concepts are *not* already revealed in the ancient writings of the Holy Writ.

Science has replaced religion as the dominant force for social structure. But many people regret that science lacks the mysticism of the old ways of looking at nature. Of all sciences, astronomy is viewed as the most "clean." It is not involved with such things as The Bomb, pollution or nerve gas. Yet, what can be more natural, but so utterly mysterious, as a falling apple? How does the apple know where the earth is? It befits scientists to be fundamentally skeptical.

"Mommy, can I stay up and watch the world come to an end?"

The wages of sin is death. The wages of evangelist Pat Robertson is $230,000,000 per year.

There is a God! ... by popular demand.---Rev. Wacko Wright

The domain of the supernatural has become ever more limited as more phenomena are rationally explained by scientific principles. In the past, humans invoked God to cause the unpredictable and viewed the world as a temperamental place, full of caprice and random occurrences. These days, theologians of the mainstream churches are inclined to disbelieve that God directly interferes with the running of the universe but only that he may have been involved in the initial creation. Ever since Copernicus demoted the earth from the center of all creation, it has become usual for scientists to assume that our place in the cosmos is in no sense privileged.

During the decade between 1957 and 1967, the science of geology was in a state of turmoil over the question of whether continents drifted or not. Oceanographers went to sea and geologists crawled over the mountains of the earth to collect facts pro or con. The controversy was won in favor of continental drift, which is now established as fact. The theory to explain drift is called *plate tectonics*, which continues in a state of development and modification. This is the method of science — the answers are changeable but only when based on compelling new evidence. In contrast, religion remains forever set in concrete. The great theological questions have remained unsettled for two thousand years as these "truths" are based upon faith which supercedes all evidence to the contrary. For example, Is Jesus God, the Son of God, or was he a man with god-like qualities? How is it best to baptize — by sprinkle, dip, or pour? How many angels can dance on the head of a pin? These questions remain unresolved and can only be answered by the sword.

Religion suppresses rational processes. Martin Luther said, "Reason is the greatest enemy of faith. It never comes to the aid of spiritual things, but struggles against the Divine Word, treating with contempt all that emanates from God." This way of thinking accounts for much that is ugly in religions. It sets heretics on fire, promotes ignorance, inflames bigotry, encourages superstition, erases history, and slaughters the opposition. There is an adoration of mystery and desire for submission.

If we invoke God's works to fill in our gaps of scientific knowledge, it puts Him in the breadline of the unemployed every time His miracles are replaced by naturalistic explanations. A science with all its problem areas bridged by miracles ceases to have any workability. The basic premise of religion is that God is unknowable even though he orders specific errands for his flock. Faith is belief without reason. The church and science are natural enemies. We live in a post-religious era, an Age of Reason. It is high time we all realize this.

Theologians are fond of saying that Albert Einstein (1870-1955) believed in God. Certainly he often spoke of God, but he explicitly stated that he believed in the God of the philosopher Spinoza. Well, Spinoza's God was Nature. Most scientists would go along with that. It is the supernatural that scientists cannot accept. If God is Nature, He is profligate. A million billion billion dollars worth of energy is expended each day by the sun and only a minute portion reaches the earth. Eventually the sun will die as the credit runs out and pays the debt with annihilation.

Aristotle maintained that everything is caused. But to complete the chain of causality, he decided that there must have been a first "uncaused" cause or "prime mover" to set the universe in motion — the clock winder, so to speak. Christian theologians of the Middle Ages seized upon this view with the Prime Mover being God. But they ignored the fact that Aristotle had explicitly rejected the idea that mind could exist apart from matter, thus ruling out the spirit world of angels, ghosts, and a personal God.

Man becomes civilized, not in proportion to his willingness to believe, but in proportion to his willingness to doubt.

Sometimes Christians are not content with turning the other cheek when one is smitten. They will bend their back and offer a wider surface for castigation.

3

THE MEANING OF DARWINISM

Evolution takes a modicum of courage to accept. Science cannot compete with science fiction and reality cannot compete with fantasy. We must tell it like it is and accept the world with no guiding hand, no personal God, no Heaven or Hell, and no everlasting life — as such wishful thinking has no place in Darwinism.

Religionists like a mystic world and they become annoyed when evolution provides an answer. Actually it tells us where we came from and even suggests where we are going. All in all, it explains too much rather than too little. But evolution is reality which sometimes is hard to accept.

Evolution is the central organizing concept of the life sciences. Why is it that fundamentalists become angry to the point of incoherence whenever evolution is mentioned? It is not that their ancestry is maligned by the evolutionary relationship between man and the anthropoid apes. Instead it would seem that evolution takes much of the mystery out of life and leaves God largely unemployed. It is no more atheistic than long division but it *does* reject Michelangelo's concept of God as an Old-Man-in-the-Sky who operates one's life on a day-to-day basis. Of course, if God is superfluous, then preachers, deacons, gurus and other members of the various God-squads in turn become unemployed. Many evolutionists remain religious but not in a simplistic way. They reject miracles and view God as ultranatural rather than supernatural.

When in doubt, trill. It's more effective than praying

The Perfect Compromise: God created Darwin and Eve.

Some aspects of life which are explained by Darwinism are: 1) The existence of two sexes — male and female; 2) The reason for birth, growth to maturity, and death. Immortality exists in our genes but not in our bodies; 3) The reason for the great sexual drive and attendant reproduction which generates variability in the offspring and fuels natural selection; 4) The fact that we do not live in a benign world but one where Nature is red of tooth and claw; 5) The earth does not belong to man, man belongs to the earth; 6) Individual life of a man has both a beginning and end, unlike creationism where life has a beginning but no end. 7) Darwinism regards man as super ape rather than a fallen angel; 8) It rejects the arrogance that the earth was created for man alone; 9) It places the survival of the species, including *Homo sapiens,* above that of the individual; 10) Unlike creationism, it does not exempt man from natural selection and survival of the fittest; 11) It does not put the chicken before the egg, or the cart before the horse, when actually the chicken is the egg's strategy for begatting another egg; and 12) Darwinism posits that virtually all men are created genetically, if not legally, unequal as we are all individuals and not clones. Except for identical twins the chances of two brothers being genetically identical is vanishingly small — only one chance in 70 billion.

Darwinism is more than just a threat to the biblical accounts of creation. Evolution threatens the entire epistemological structure of fundamentalism. A spherical earth rather than the biblical flat world, they could adapt to that. But evolution, No! In the creationists distorted view we are left to choose between the bible versus science, faith versus evidence, darkness versus light, and the Dark Ages versus the Renaissance. To believe in evolution, they aver, is like shooting the Easter Bunny. Evolution may not provide the best of all possible worlds but it has commanded recognition because it illuminates the human condition and displays a prodigious power of performance and prediction.

UNIFIED FIELD THEORY

In the beginning there was Aristotle,
And objects at rest tended to remain at rest,
And objects in motion tended to come to rest,
And soon everything was at rest,
And God saw that it was boring.

Then God created Newton,
And objects at rest tended to remain at rest,
But objects in motion tended to remain in motion,
And energy was conserved and momentum was conserved and matter was conserved,
And God saw that it was conservative.

Then God created Einstein,
And everything was relative,
And fast things became short,
And straight things became curved,
And the universe was filled with inertial frames,
And God saw that it was relatively general, but some of it was especially relative.

Then God created Bohr,
And there was the principle,
And the principle was quantum,
And all things were quantified,
But some things were still relative,
And God saw that it was confusing.

Then God was going to create Furgeson,
And Furgeson would have unified,
And he would have fielded a theory,
And all would have been one,
But it was the seventh day,
And God rested,
And objects at rest tend to remain at rest.
            —Tim Joseph, *copyright N.Y. Times Co., reprinted by permission*

If "War is Hell", I know of a lot of people who ought to go to war.

4

RELIGION AND WAR: HOLY WAR, HOLY TERROR

For a thousand years, science and religion have been at war. Scientists, however, do not realize that the conflict is on, and so they are losing. New religious lunacy has broken out, and the crazies are at the gate. The ability to think freely and critically is the best defense against tyranny. Subscribing to absolutism, zealots do not realize that values can be relative. Rationality and humanism are fading out.

As each day passes, the world grows more destabilized. The chief culprits are the religious zealots — the Ghadafis, the Khomenis, the Sikhs, etc. The gap between the advanced countries and the Third World is opening and the latter tend to opt for theocracy. Technological progress involves the very small elite, which is vastly outnumbered by *hoi polloi*. With their vast numerical superiority, it is easy to believe that these mobs might take over and dominate the world.

It is said that money is not everything, but is way ahead of whatever is in second place. The same can be said for the population explosion as a destabilizing force. But according to creationists, this is a non-problem because God will consummate His plan of Armageddon before humans become numerous enough to become a threat.

Our galaxy, the Milky Way, contains about ten billion stars and it is reasonably supposed that many may have planets where life could have evolved. One estimate places that number of such planets at one million. One must assume that some of this intelligent life must be as advanced as that on earth, and in some cases even more so. The question arises: "Where is everybody?" — why haven't they found us or at least communicated electronically? The explanation would seem to be that "intelligence" is inherently programmed to self-destruct. On earth we observe that as technology advances, our world becomes ever more destabilized. And the cause is religion.

Religion is the root of all terrorism. This is an obvious trueism but it is never aired on TV when the pundits wring their hands in frustration every time Palestinian shi-ites hijack a jet airplane, a ship, take a hostage, or whatever. Any discussion of religion is taboo. Fanatical devotion to religious causes leads to rabid proselytizing, emotional instability and acts of terrorism. Thus we have the vivisection of Lebanon, Ireland, and British India (first by the Moslems and now by the Sikhs). The threat of a nuclear holocaust comes not from the non-theistic USSR but from the fundamentalist theocracies like Iran.

Religion: The cause of wars.

The supposed biblical prediction of the great battle of Armageddon claims that the world is about to suffer a nuclear holocaust involving the armies of the east (Chinese), the armies of the north (Soviet Union) and the armies of the west (Europe and U.S.A.). The only escapees will be those who have accepted Jesus, for they will be raptured before the period of tribulation. This belief in the inevitability of nuclear war is a destabilizing influence.

The theology of Armageddon identifies our nation's enemies as enemies of God. Its subscribers believe that the destruction of these enemies is decreed in the Holy Writ. They conclude that reconciliation with America's adversaries is ultimately futile, and that a nuclear war is winnable. Hence, there is religious and theological justification for the pre-emptive use of nuclear weapons. Armageddon remains a cornerstone of fundamentalism.

President Reagan on a number of occasions has indicated that he believes that the Armageddon prophecies of the Bible are coming true. But he also has added that his interest is philosophical, and that such ideas are not a part of military planning. Mainstream religion leaders call "Armageddon theology" a heresy and they urge political leaders to renounce it. Jewish leaders also regard it as a distortion of biblical writings, and they add, "We should know, for after all, we wrote the Bible." But the evangelists continue to rant and rave about Armageddon — so much so that it could become a self-fulfilling prophecy.

The religious conflicts of today and throughout history are simply skirmishes in the unending Great War Between Science and Religion. It began with victories for science by Greeks and Romans, (Aristotle, Archimedes, etc.), but this ancient age of enlightenment was overcome around A.D. 300 by the rise of Christiandom which plunged the world in the Dark Ages for a millenium. With the Renaissance science once again attained the upper hand. But the war goes on, and lately the armies of the night are once again establishing theocracies throughout the world. Those naive persons who see some accommodation or convergence between science and religion are simply whistling Dixie. Never shall it be ! — at least not until Hell freezes over and the Pope becomes a Mormon.

Seventy-two Nobel Prize Winners Oppose Creationism:
(Washington, AP, 8/16/86) Seventy-two American winners of the Nobel Prize in Science urged the Supreme Court to strike down a Louisiana law requiring public schools teaching evolution to teach creationism as well. In a brief filed with the high court, the Nobel laureates and 24 scientific organizations argued that the "creation-science" mentioned in the state law is really religion and has no place in science classes. "Teaching religious ideas mislabeled as science is detrimental to scientific education: It sets up a false conflict between science and religion and misleads our youth about the nature of scientific inquiry," the friend-of-the-court brief stated. This is the largest group of Nobel laureates ever to support a single statement on any subject. Stephen J. Gould, professor of paleontology at Harvard University, called creation-science "just a phony new legal strategy" in an effort to get around past court rulings banning religious inculcation.

Life after Death
Yes, there truly is life after death! In fact there is a whole kingdom of life —the Kingdom of the Fungi. When any member of the other biological kingdoms (the Monera, Protista, Plantae and Animalia) die; the fungi take over reducing the organic constituents to a form which can be assimilated by other life. Fungi play an essential role in the recycling process permitting life to go on. Halelujah Nature!

Convinced that there is no eternal life awaiting him, man will strive all the more to brighten his life on earth and rationally improve his condition in harmony with that of his fellows. --- Ernst Haeckel

5

POPULATION BOMB

The world's worst problem is the population explosion. In fact, of the ten most pressing problems, it is numbers one through nine. A stable global population would be the initial step in saving mankind. But so long as we have clergymen and popes who proclaim "go forth and multiply", there is no hope for us. The problem is real and the choices are hard, but states of innocence are reserved for the Garden of Eden.

Man, unfortunately, is no longer subjected to survival of the fittest but often, it seems, to be survival of the unfittest. Blacks with Ph.D degrees average 1.6 children per family, while blacks in the ghetto beget an average of 6 children. Much of the world is already overpopulated. In China there is a thrust for negative population growth by permitting only one child per family. Let's hope that we in the United States are never subjected to such rigorous solutions. An average of 2.3 children per family would result in zero population growth.

Too many animals or people are not a laughing matter. Overpopulation is making every major problem we face more difficult to solve. Too many people are the basic cause of poverty, environmental degradation, etc., and behind the population explosion is religion. The overpopulated Third World countries are the ones most likely to trigger the nuclear holocaust, rather than the U.S.S.R., and bring on the nuclear winter wiping out our civilization. The growth of a rational and intelligent populace cannot keep pace with the rabbit-like propagation of the ignorant.

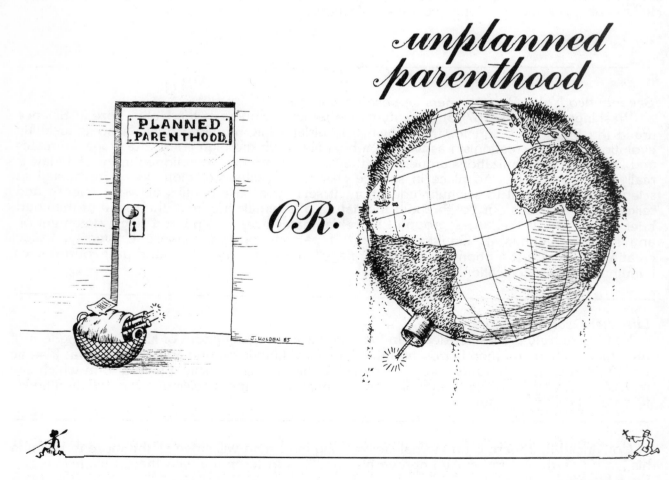

If the sun were created to light and heat the earth, what a waste of energy! We receive only one two thousand-millionth part of the solar radiation.

The biblical directive to "multiply and replenish" made sense in the early history of man but not today. We are short of tigers, elephants and eagles but not people. As Malthus emphasized, the resources of the earth are limited while our reproductive ability is not. We cannot multiply without paying the ultimate price. There are already enough overpopulated countries — India, China, Mexico, etc. Mexico City is projected to have 30 million inhabitants ("the Pope's children") by the year 2,000. But no city can contain this many people so they will swarm north like locusts. Each night "wetbacks" swarm across our border from Brownsville, Texas, to San Diego, California. The influx will continue to grow because of Mexico's church-promoted baby boom. There are now more children under the age of fifteen in Mexico than in the United States.

The ultimate solution, according to some, is to blast our surplus people off to inhabit Mars or some other planet. But, as populations grow, nations become ever weaker and resource poor. An overpopulated Earth, like India, would be unable to afford high technology. The human populaion of more than four billion is a blighted asset. Some 25 percent of the 100 million babies now born each year will be physically and mentally stunted by malnutrition and poverty. Overpopulation, illiteracy and ignorance are epidemic in many countries of the world today. Spaceship Earth is careening through the void with an assortment of religious zealots fighting for the controls. Their chances improve as our numbers increase. The Great Unwashed are urged to "go forth and multiply". The future is bleak. Even the most advanced nations are taking no effective action toward birth control or zero population growth. It is well to remember, that doing nothing is equally making a decision. Self-destruction by "pop-pollution" is in the offing.

"There's always room for one more."
—Mother Theresa

INDIA
PACKED BY TRADITION, DOGMA AND BLIND FAITH
A PRODUCT OF IGNORANCE

"With God on our side we shall, with our good German sword, conquer our enemies", said Kaiser Wilhelm.

"The dear God has fought with my armies so faithfully," said the Emperor of Austria-Hungary.

"Remember, my soldiers, when you are in battle, God is always with you," said the Czar of Russia.

"If my efforts were crowned with success, it is due to God's gracious guidance," said Field Marshall von Hindenburg.

God, it seems, is on everybody's side -- but only one side wins.

6

The Bible is one of twenty-seven books for which divine origin is claimed. Christians deny the divinity of all bibles but their own. We deny the divinity of only one more than they do.

Out of 250 Jewish-Christian writings, sixty-six have arbitrarily been declared canonical by Protestants. The rejected books are of the same general character as those now published together as "The Holy Bible." Circumstances rather than merit determined selection.

For 150 years the Christian Bible consisted of the sacred books of the Jews. The New Testament was not formed until the latter half of the second century, when Irenaeus selected twenty books from among forty or more gospels, nearly as many acts of apostles, a score of revelations, and a hundred epistles. Why were these particular books chosen? Why four gospels instead of one? Irenaeus: "There are four quarters of the earth in which we live and four universal winds." The Gospels were unknown to Peter, Paul, and the early Church Fathers. They were forged later.

The Bible did not assume anything like its present form until the fourth century. The Roman Catholic, Greek Catholic, and Protestant canons were not adopted until modern times. The Bible was recognized as a collection of independent writings. The Council of Trent (1563) determined the Roman Catholic canon consisting of seventy-two books. The romanists anathematize the Protestant Bible, and the Protestants denounce the Catholic Bible as a "popish imposture." The Greek Catholics at the Council of Jerusalem in 1672 finally accepted Revelation. Their Bible contains several books not in the Roman canon. The Westminister Assembly in 1647 approved the list of sixty-six books composing the Authorized Version, the one most used in America. Our Bible, therefore, is less than 300 years old. Adoption was by majority vote.

Charles Smith
American Editor

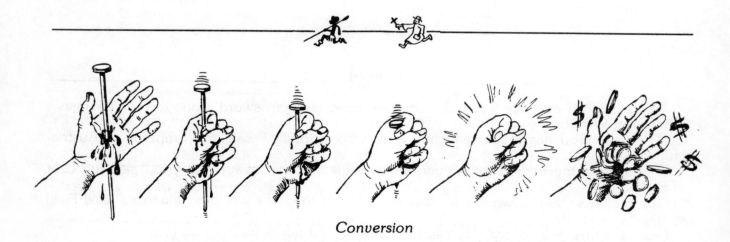

Conversion

7

DEFINITIONS OF GOD

It has been said that if you are asked if you believe in God, the most confusing answer you can give is, Yes. No two people will agree on any definition. Albert Einstein spoke of God almost as much as Ronald Reagan. When pressed to be specific he said that he believed in the God of Spinoza. This philosopher's God was Nature. But the "natural supernatural" is an oxymoron — a contradiction of terms.

God: To Moses from the burning bush: "I AM WHO I AM," (Exodus 3:13-14). The only definition within the bible by God himself.

* * * * *

God: Almighty, eternal, holy, immortal, immense, immutable, incomprehensible, ineffable, infinite, invisible, just, loving, merciful, most high, most wise, omnipotent, omniscient, omnipresent, patient, perfect, provident, supreme, and true. —National Catholic Almanac.

* * * * *

God: The supremely Unknowable known only by supreme ignorance through true faith... —St. Maximus the Confessor, Greek 7th Century.

* * * * *

God: Hydrogen — cosmologist's definition.

* * * * *

God: Existant...by popular demand.

* * * * *

God: A Santa Claus for adults.

* * * * *

God: A supernatural and transcendent being unbounded by natural laws and hence capable of miracles. Webster's Dictionary.

* * * * *

God: A being that is incapable of being characterized, is nothing in particular, and hence victorious by definition.

* * * * *

God: Superstrings in ten dimensional space, coiled around the magic number 496 — Mathematicians definition.

* * * * *

God: The Great I Am, all-seeing, all acting, all loving, all wise, and eternal; principle, mind, soul, spirit, life, truth, love, overall and all. (I guess that about wraps it up!) — Mary Baker Eddy, founder of Christian Science.

* * * * *

God: The Inexplicable invoked to elucidate the Unexplainable. A delightful whimsy which people understandably are loath to part with. After all, no one wants to shoot Santa Claus.

In their next prayer, creationists might implore God to grant them an education, so that they will not remain ignorant all of their lives. --- Isaac Asimov

Men will never be free until the last king is strangled with the entrails of the last priest.--- Denis Diderot (1713-1784)

Where knowledge ends, religion begins.---Benjamin Disraeli (1804-1881)

8

GOD: THE GREAT DESIGNER?

The classic proof of the existence of a supernatural being is the argument from design. The idea goes back to Marcus Tullius Cicero's *De Natura Deorum* of 77 B.C. He wrote that design proved the existence of the Roman pagan gods. A design requires great designers — gods. In the Christian Era, this line of reasoning was first formalized in 1802 by William Paley, Bishop of Wearmouth, in England. In his treatise, "Natural Theology: Evidences of the Existence and Attributes of the Deity Collected from the Appearances of Nature." Paley wrote: "In crossing a heath...suppose I found a watch upon the ground...it is inevitable that the watch must have had a maker; that there must have existed at some time at some place or other, an artificer or artificers, who formed it for some purpose. Who comprehended its construction and designed its use? In short, a design requires a designer, and great designs such as man, the earth, or the universe require God."

This appears to be convincing evidence for God, but there is a fallacy in this logic. Any watchmaker had parents, and these parents in turn had parents ad infinitum. So it would seem that God necessarily had parents — and that these God-parents had God-parents ad infinitum. In Judaeo-Christian theology God was created ex-nihilo (and asexually). It follows that God's-parent who sparked him into existence must have had ever greater power than God himself. Therefore the trail to the beginning, from Man to God and to God-parents is a progression to the Infinitely Great in the infinite past. This is The Problem!

Evolution avoids The Problem. Evolutionists accept that any watchmaker had parents and these parents in turn had parents ad infinitum. But each parent is lesser, not greater, than its offspring (in an evolutionary scheme) so that down the vast corridors of time, life forms become ever simpler. It is a matter of regression not progression from Man, early man, primates, primitive mammals, reptiles, amphibians, fish, ... to the first cell, or first replicating entity, perhaps a strand of RNA. Thus there is an infinite regression to essentially zero — the beginning of Life. There is no Problem.

Watches, paintings and Mt. Rushmore, of course, imply an intelligent designer. But the fallacy of God the Designer is that any intelligent designer, either God or man, must in turn have had parents.

The *Design,* or teleological, argument posits that there is an observable structure to the universe which required a designer—God. This implies that one can identify objects of God's design in the same way we identify objects of man's design — e.g. a watch. But the argument is circular because the presumption of divine design must be based on examples of things not divinely designed. For example, if we found a watch or a computer on Mars we would expect the presence of intelligent life. But if we discovered only bacteria, this would not be evidence of intelligent things. We determine whether or not something was designed by the fact that it differs from natural things. Hence, if man is a natural thing, he was not designed.

The *First Cause,* or cosmological, argument for a deity posits that every effect requires a sufficient cause. The universe is an effect and therefore must have a cause—God. But what or who caused God? Unless one posits other gods, we are left with an initial effect without any cause. Additionally, there is no reason to suppose that an uncaused first cause still exists. It, He or She, may be defunct or dead. If so, why pray? Theists assert that God is a supernatural and trancendent being. But a being without natural existence does not have any comprehensible existence. To exist is to be something rather than nothing and to be something specific. But to assign definite characteristics to God is to limit his abilities. So theists introduce such attributes as eternal, immortal, immutable, infinite, invisible, all-loving, omnipotent, omniscient, omnipresent, perfect and supreme. These terms really say nothing about what God is, only what he is not. To say that he is immutable means only that he does not change. To say that he is invisible means only that he is not visible. With such negative attributes he cannot be distinguished from nothing. For, while God does not change, nor does nothing. God is not visible, nor is nothing.

Theological Evolution, although accepted by many Catholics and mainstream Protestants, is detested by Creationists. Theological evolution is the belief that in the beginning God started the evolutionary ball rolling and then let Nature take over. This, of course, leaves Him largely unemployed today. But they can fall back on the God-of-the-Gaps concept, where He is invoked to explain all as yet unexplained mysteries. To their annoyance, science continues day by day to solve these mysteries with natural explanations. God's workload is becoming even smaller and His unemployment is in the offing.

Creationists resort to the supernatural because they are faced with a mystery they cannot solve — i.e., the Origin of Life. Science is full of unsolved mysteries but the scientist must await sufficient data. The creationist, on the other hand, feels the need to solve the problem without data. This he does by positing another mystery — the mystery of the Supernatural. We end up with two mysteries instead of just one.

The family that preys together, stays together.

QUOTES FROM JOSEPH LEWIS

In the town of Cholula, which has a population of only 12,000 people, there were three hundred and sixty-five churches--one for every day of the year! The officials of the present Mexican government are trying to determine what the people did on the extra day provided by Leap Year. Mind you, three hundred and sixty-five churches, but not a single public school or a hospital in a town of 12,000 people!

When Lincoln ran for Congress against the Reverend Peter Cartwright, charges were brought against him (Lincoln) by clergymen that he was an infidel, and that he said that Christ was an illegitimate child. And not once did Lincoln deny the truth of these charges. When asked why he did not deny them, Lincoln said he did not do so for two reasons: First, he knew the charges to be true; and second, they could be easily proved.

Slavery is just as much a fundamental part of the Bible as is the Virgin Birth. (See Leviticus 25:44-46; Timothy 1:6; and Titus 2.9:)

When the Church can no longer crush the skull of a Hypatia; imprison a Galileo or burn a Bruno; and when it can no longer excommunicate a Spinoza or banish a Voltaire, a truly great victory will have been won.

The history of the human race during that period known as the "Dark Age" was written with the blood that dripped from the sword of the Church.

Letter to Oral Roberts:

Dear Oral Roberts, An undated letter to me bearing your signature reads that through your ministry: "...a little girl doomed to the life of a cripple is whole! a man received his sight! a boy threw away his crutches! and hearing is restored to the deaf!..." Now, I do not believe a single word...and I brand you a deliberate and unconscionable liar...The Courts have already decided that fraud cannot be practiced under the cloak of religion... (Continued on Next Page)

129

You say "God needs you" meaning, of course, send in money. But what does God need you for? Is not He already an Omnipotent, All Powerful, Infinite Being?...When the book, *The Power of the Charlatan* is rewritten, you deserve a special chapter entitled: *The Prince of Humbug*...

You say: "If you love money and keep making money and you can't ever make enough, then you are in Hell." I have a financial report on your condition--and how you must enjoy Hell!..

If you can cure the blind, as you say you have done, what need is there for them to read your sermons in Braille...I demand that you produce one of your "miracles" today...in broad daylight where honest men can witness it...As Shakespeare would say, "What an odious and damned lie!" ---Joseph Lewis

THE BLIND WATCHMAKER

The strongest argument for the existence of God is the argument from design. Wherever there is a watch, the argument runs, there must have been a watchmaker. You can take all the pieces of a watch, place them in a box and shake it forever, and you will never get a watch. And a whirlwind will never sweep through a junkyard and create a Boeing 747. How, then, could the complexity we see in man have come about by chance?

All appearances to the contrary, life can, and has, evolved from the simple to the complex. Given enough time, and enough chances, through mutations and natural selection, the improbable becomes the probable — and in fact, the certainty. Evolution is a blind watchmaker who leaves God unemployed. Like it or not, this is the real world.

Lest there be any scrap of doubt about evolution, readers do have in me an atheist reviewer. Whatever the "resurgence" of religion, this is still, thanks to Jefferson and Madison, an uncensored newspaper in a free country. And even if I am wrong and there is a God, and even if he has nothing better to do than to think about me, he cannot possibly hate me for my views. After all, he gave me a logical and rational brain, and this brain looks around, weighs the evidence and concludes that evolution is right...

Excerpt from a review by Lee Dembart of *The Blind Watchmaker: Why the Evidence of Evolution Reveals a Universe Without Design,* by Richard Dawkins.

"Send me your poor, your tired, your huddled masses yearning to be free..."

And your illiterate
And your illegal
And your simpletons
And your criminals
And your terrorists
And your diseased
And your...

10

U.S.A. NOT FOUNDED ON CHRISTIANITY

It pleases many Americans to believe that our government is founded on Christianity. However, the Treaty of Tripoli of 1797 ending the Barbary Coast War (Miller, 1931) states:

> As the government of the United States of America is not in any sense founded on the Christian religion, — as it has in itself no character of enmity against the laws, religion or tranquility of Musselmen, — and as the said States never have entered into any war or act of hostility against any Mehomitan nation, it is declared by the parties that no pretext arising from religious opinion shall ever produce an interruption of the harmony existing between the two countries.

By what it does say, the constitution makes the same point. Its preamble aims exclusively at secular goals in aiming "to form a more perfect union, establish justice, insure domestic tranquility, provide for the common defense, promote the general welfare, and secure the blessings of liberty to ourselves and our posterity." Moreover, the main body of the Constitution does not name, presuppose, nor acknowledge any deity. Neither does it mention nor acknowledge any divine law above the laws passed by Congress and upheld by the Supreme Court. Furthermore, the Constitution utilizes neither biblical language nor theological concepts. Neither prayer nor any ritual act is mentioned or recommended. In short, this thoroughtly secular instrument of government has nothing to do with a kingdom not of this world... Delos McKnown, philosopher.

What was the first sin ever committed? It was the sin of believing on faith alone without evidence. If Eve had not been a credulous fool, she would not have transgressed by eating the apple from the tree of knowledge.

Who was the first divine who preached about God and immortality? It was Satan! He told people that they need not die but could have everlasting life in heaven and be as gods. A damnable lie for God himself hath declared: "Dust thou art, and unto dust shalt thou return."

SECULAR HUMANISM

Secularism is a good thing; without it the modern world as we know it would be impossible. The Secular Humanist Declaration in 1980 listed ten concepts of secularism: (1) The right to free inquiry. (2) Separation of church and state. (3) The ideal of individual and democratic freedom. (4) Ethics based on critical intelligence instead of supernatural pronouncement. (5) Moral education can and should be cultivated in children apart from religion, for example, in the public schools. (6) The cultivation of religious skepticism — and, indeed, skepticism toward any unproven assertions. (7) The commitment to give priority to reason and truth arrived at rationally. (8) The recognition of the scientific method as the most trustworthy way of knowing. (9) The acceptance of evolution and its constant testing and refinement. (10) A commitment to universal education and literacy.

Secular humanism, like science, is an open door that invites inquiry, debate, and verification. It abhors finality. Religion is a belief system in which the door is closed. The devotee merely believes in faith and is actively discouraged from questioning doctrine. A Department of Education should not be a "Ministry of Truth." The mission of religious schools is to indoctrinate while that of secular schools is to educate — with an open door to let the fresh air in.

In the process of evolution most "new" structures are modifications of pre-existing ones. The entire body of knowledge of comparative anatomy supports this observation. The design of animals shows an incredible conservatism. The limbs of all vertebrates have the same set of component bones and muscles, yet they perform diverse functions. Isn't it remarkable that nature has never invented the wheel? As Darwin observed, "Nature is prodigal in variety but niggardly in invention."

"Yes, I will accept the burden of the poor if you stop creating them."

I know that God exists because it is impossible---Tertullian (ca. 200 A.D.)

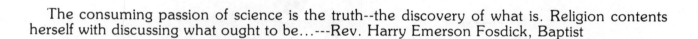

The consuming passion of science is the truth--the discovery of what is. Religion contents herself with discussing what ought to be...---Rev. Harry Emerson Fosdick, Baptist

The theist and the scientist are rival interpreters of nature. The one retreats as the other advances.---Joseph McCabe

One touch of Darwin makes the whole world kin.---George Bernard Shaw

12

RE: HURRICANES, SECULAR HUMANISM, AND GOD

In 1900 when an unannounced hurricane struck Galveston, Texas, 6000 persons died. Then Florida lost 1800 in an unpredicted 1928 hurricane; Audrey claimed 550 in 1957; Camille killed 250 in 1969; and Agnes killed 122 in 1972. Despite variables, it is easy to see that storm fatalities have decreased with time since 1900 as the science of forecasting has progressed. No one can estimate how many were saved during the ravages of hurricanes Elena and Gloria when only 20 died.

This is what secular humanism is all about. Meteorologists at the National Hurricane Center in Miami used science rather than theology or black magic to predict the intensity, course and landfall of these killer storms. Coastline residents were ordered to evacuate, saving many lives through *human intervention*. Ironically, many of those saved thanked "God".

Here we have an example of secular (non-religious, of this world, scientific) humanism (man-centered, for human benefit) in action. If the "Billy Grahams" of this world are correct in suggesting that natural disasters are "God's will", then hurricane watchers were thwarting God.

(When Mt. Etna erupted recently, Italian priests prayed and wafted incense in a pitiful effort to stay the encroaching lava flows. In contrast, when lava threatened to inundate the Haimey fishing village in the Freisan Islands, the secular-minded Icelanders broke out their fire hoses and froze the molten rock).

Not surprisingly, the fundamentalists have refrained from labeling hurricane watchers as secular humanists. But is this not exactly what they are? (Excerpt from the Secular Humanists Bulletin).

"God be with you!"

134

13

GLOSSARY

Awe: A religious precept by which one bows to things not understood.

Cartesian: Of or pertaining to Rene Decartes, originator of the X Y Z coordinates of geometry and the timeless dictum *Cogito ergo sum* (I think, therefore I am). Actually this was a misprint of *Coito ergo sum*. By his own admission Decartes was a human encyclopedia, and the first and last person to know everything there was to be known — or at least he thinked he thought. Less known is his later observation: *Cogito ergo spud* (I think, therefore I yam).

Chronus Nexus: The brief, fleeting, and instantaneous moment in the history of a country when the ascending Catholic Church achieves a 51 percent majority of the population through miscalculations in the workings of papal roulette, and just before the achievement of 99 percent Catholic plurality. This occurred in Italy in 1452, Spain in 1320, and Ireland in 1582. For the U.S.A., the anticipated date is 1996.

*Cogito Ergo Spud
(I think, therefore
I yam)*

Church of England: A place where an atheist can feel comfortable.

Dark Ages: A dismal period in history from 300 to 800 A.D. when little or nothing much (mostly nothing) happened, and civilization stagnated. The beginning of the Dark Ages was synchronous with the establishment of the Christian Church. Historians agree in a direct relationship, but disagree as to whether religion was the cause or the effect of the Dark Ages.

Ellis' Law: Named after Dr. Robert Ellis, a psychotherapist. This law states, "Religious indoctrination creates people who are inflexible, dogmatic and bigoted. Either religion appeals to the stupid or religion results in stupid people." Its reality is supported by the inverse correlation between IQ scores and religiosity.

Fear: Phobia, for example: hierophobia (fear of priests), hagiophobia (saints), papaphobia (the Pope), demonophobia (demons), phasmophobia (ghosts), pneumatophobia (spirits), uranophobia (heaven), stygiophobia (hell), agyrophobia (crossing a street), apeirophobia (infinity), phronemophobia (thinking), and phobophobia (fear of fear) and little things that go bump in the night.

Macroevolution:

   It sounds like a child's riddle: What do you get when you cross a firefly with a tobacco plant? Answer: tobacco that lights itself. But this is essentially what geneticists did in 1986 at the University of California in San Diego. By outfitting a fragment of the plant virus with the gene that tells firefly cells to produce a protein central to generating phosphorescent light, the scientists created a tobacco plant that glows in the dark. It is an example of virtuoso genetic engineering, and of a *macro-evolutionary* jump which creationists claim to be impossible.

> If the ignorance of nature gave birth to gods, the knowledge of nature is calculated to destroy them.---Baron D'Holbach

> In the name of religion human blood has flowed since the time of the first Christian Emperor, Constantine. The churches by vain, ambitious, and hypocritical disputes have ravaged Europe, Asia, and Africa...The Christian religion has destroyed half the human race. May we return to Nature whose declared enemy religion is. Then the world will be composed of good citizens, just fathers, obedient children and tender friends. Nature has given us *this* religion in giving us reason. May fanaticism pervert it no more! I die filled with this desire.---John Meslier, Catholic Priest, Etrepigny, France, 1732.

Geologist: A scientist who walks on water by knowing where the rocks are.

Gurus: Divines, shamen, deacons, reverends, priests, medicine men, warlocks, dowsers, jujus, necromancers, sorcerers, dervishes, obeah men, yogi, voodoos, witches and fools who practice the black arts of thaumaturgy and omphaloskepsis. They successfully exacerbate curable diseases while puzzling each other.

Heathen: A benighted creature who has the folly to worship something he can see and feel. --- A. Bierce

Holy Ghost: Intentional inexistence and presence in absence. His Nondescript Holiness.

Indefinition: De-defining words so that they are intentionally vague, fuzzy and indefinite. A cardinal sin among scientists, who pride themselves on being precise, but a virtue among creationists who desire to confuse rather than elucidate. They term evolution as a religion and a theory as a guess. And the word God is another example. It is a concept so broad and inclusive that covers everything in general but nothing in particular. Creationists downplay language and upgrade the limbic system at the expense of the cerebral cortex. Theirs is an unconscionable corruption of the language. "The question is," said Alice, "whether you can make a word mean so many different things." But it is not so much a matter of *Alice in Wonderland* as it is *Malice in Blunderland*.

Sturgeon's Law

One of the basic truths of the universe is, according to Sturgeon's Law, that "95 percent of everything is nonsense." Added to this is Dembart's Corollary which states that there is a dominant gene in man's make up causing people to believe the 95 percent of foolishness rather than the 5 percent of reality. Belief in nonsense takes many forms: spiritualism, astrology, faith healing, and above all religion. Naive belief systems are fueled by a craving to know the unknown. Fairy tales are invented and believed.

Ad:
Did you know that through a modern miracle of medicine, you can double the population of India every night? Send in $19.95 now for information to Every-Sperm-Is-Sacred, Inc. 666 Backwater St., Improvidence, R.I., 24680. And that every cell in your body has a soul? Clone yourself--and let your clone do all the scut work. Mail in a fingernail clipping. Include $99.99 and bus fare. Send-in-the-Clones, Inc., 12 Hallelujah Dr., Big Wow, OK, 22666.

If indeed the world in which we live has been produced in accordance with a Plan, we shall have to reckon Nero a saint in comparison with the Author of that Plan. Fortunately, however, the evidence of Divine Purpose is non-existent; so at least one must infer from the fact that no evidence is adduced by those who believe in it. We are, therefore, spared the necessity for that attitude of impotent hatred which every brave and humane man would otherwise be called upon to adopt toward the Almighty Tyrant. ---Bertrand Russell

---

To the Greeks the four elements were air, water, fire, and earth; to the evangelist the four elements are wind, brimstone, smoke and hot air. I think one should add peanut butter.
—Ichabod Balderdash

(Comment regarding clergy) Their nonsense suits His nonsense. ---Charles II, King of England, 1665.

136

Leger-de-main: An emaciated French thaumaturgist who once invited Fata Morgana to Maxim's for a sumptuous repast of unicorn steak *a la truffle*, topped with Flim Flam *a la maison*. He skillfully jerked the table cloth from under the feast, spilling only one glass of Perrier.

Mammon: The God of the world's leading religion. His chief temples are the towers of Wall Street. --- A. Bierce

Metaphysics: The art of befuddling one's self methodically. --- James Jeans, British astronomer

Miracle: The bastard child of Faith and Reason which neither parent can afford to acknowledge.

Occam's Razor: The principle of simplicity or KISS (Keep It Simple Stupid) first enunciated in the 13th century by the Bishop of Occam who advised: *Non sunt multiplicanda entia praetor necessitatem* (Do not multiply entities beyond necessity). This principle is an anathema to theologians, metaphysicians, and shamen who prefer pronouncements garbed in garbled complexities.

Orthodox: A sinful ox, domesticated, imprisoned, and enslaved by a religious yoke. --- A. Bierce

Pragmatism: A philosophy holding that the truth is pre-eminently to be tested by the practical consequences of belief. The art of the possible as compared to religion — the science of the impossible.

Preacher: A preying, praying, prying, purveyor of pious, pasturized platitudes. A pompous panderer of parochial, pontifical piffle.

Scapegoat: In an ancient Jewish ritual, a chief priest on the Day of Atonement who, for a fee of one goat, laid the sins of penitent upon the head of a second goat and dispatched the beast to die in the wilderness (Leviticus 16). An acute shortage of goats ensued so, at the beginning of the Christian era, Jesus of Nazareth offered himself as a surrogate for the goats. The use of various scapegoats, bearing the blame for the real or imagined sins or misdeeds of others has persisted down through the ages. Recently the Jews themselves unwillingly became the scapegoats of Adolf Hitler. To spare human suffering, the theologian, Thaddeus Bombast, has campaigned for once again using goats, now in plentiful supply, as an addendum to the Geneva Convention.

Scientology: A new "church" founded by L. Ron Hubbard, author of the 1950 book *Dianetics* which explains how to "clear" yourself of "engrams". Successful praxis of this mystical procedure is attested to by the realization of a profit of $350 million without the necessity of Scientology being either a *science* or an *ology*.

Sunday: The day given over by Americans to wishing that they themselves were dead and in Heaven, and that their neighbors were dead and in hell. --- H.L. Menken

Terror: (1) Intense, overpowering fear. Anything that instills such fear. (2) Violence toward private citizens, public property and political enemies promoted by a political group to achieve or maintain supremacy. (3) An annoying or intolerable pest; nuisance. Often used in the phrase "a holy terror".

Teleologist: A word-juggling mystic who is forever seeing "wisdom" where there is none and who tries to explain the universe in terms of a presiding intelligence.

Werewolf: One of the many disguises of Satan. A werewolf relegated to the plu-perfect subjunctive. Hence, a wolf that once was, used to be, was sometimes, or if not, might be.

—The End—

NOTES

CHURCH